COUNTRY HEARTS

*A Gallery
of Country People*

COUNTRY HEARTS

A Gallery
of Country People

FRED J. TAYLOR

With illustrations by Ted Andrews

COLT BOOKS
Cambridge

COLT BOOKS LTD
9 Clarendon Road
Cambridge CB2 2BH
tel 01223 357047   fax 01223 365866

First published by Colt Books 2001

Jacket illustration by permission of *Saga Publication Ltd*

Designed by Clare Byatt

ISBN 0 905899 22 9

A catalogue record for this book is available from the
British Library

Printed in Great Britain by Biddles Ltd, www.Biddles.co.uk

Contents

The author, about 1940

Introduction

A long lifetime, spent, for the most part of it, pursuing
country sports, fishing in many corners of the world and gathering the annual harvests supplied by Nature every season,
has brought me into contact with a host of different characters.
My life has been enriched as a result and since that life has
now passed its allotted span of three score years and ten, it
is perhaps fitting that some of that richness should be shared.

Most of those I have met have been conservationists with
a respect for their quarry and an eye to the future. They have
cropped without being greedy and have never, to my
knowledge, put any species in danger of extinction.

It cannot be denied that their annual harvests have
involved the killing of game, wildfowl, fish and vermin. Nor
could it be denied that they killed for sport as well as for the
table. What has to be made clear at all times is that they took
no pleasure in the actual killing.

Protecting the lesser species from predation was undertak-
en at all times and this may have invalidated the claim that
they were hunters who ate all they killed.

In the eyes of a good conservationist, however, foxes,
mink and crows etc. have to be controlled. When numbers
are too high and other edible quarry is suffering as a result,
the hunter/conservationist believes it is essential to protect
his or her quarry. He does *not*, however, derive a sadistic
pleasure out of killing any creature for killing's sake (as all
the opponents of field sports never stop suggesting), nor
does he ever behave in a deliberately cruel fashion. He never
takes one second longer than is absolutely essential to
dispatch quarry and although accidents happen and game is
sometimes wounded, it can be truthfully said that it is never
with intent.

I was once asked at a Forum whether I enjoyed being cruel. My reply was that I could find a million ways of being cruel without venturing into the sporting field. The very meaning of the word "sporting", in my own opinion, is behaving in a decent manner and having a respect for my quarry. The fact that I have every intention of killing it does not detract from these sentiments at all.

I see no difference between the shooting of a pheasant and the beheading of a broiler chicken. Both, in terms of life and death, are identical acts. Mistakes are made on both sides and it can be said without fear of contradiction that the *instant* death of *every* creature on *either side of the fence* can never be guaranteed. Mistakes are never made with intent to cause suffering and therein lies the difference between decent behaviour and deliberate cruelty.

If I needed to introduce a regular practice that involves cruelty of the worst kind I would simply quote the deep sea fishing industry. It would be a deliberate ploy to provoke on my part but who would dare argue that the hauling up of fish from the depths of the ocean and gutting them while still alive does not involve cruelty?

At least the trout I catch are dispatched swiftly with a priest before they are gilled and gutted!

I once asked a biologist, whose job involved the killing and dissecting of small animals, if he enjoyed his job. He assured me that he did.

"So," I said, "you actually enjoy killing little animals?"

It was a wicked wind-up on my part but as he had previously accused me of killing for pleasure, it was an attempt also to bring logic back into the argument and to debate without emotion.

I introduce these minor topics to illustrate exactly where I stand in terms of field sports. I take the overall picture and study it in terms of conservation. I know, for instance, that while fox hunting and grouse shooting remain, neither species is likely to become endangered. Grouse would survive without being shot at for as long as the moors were keepered and burned off to encourage the new growth to

2

emerge. Left to themselves they would become woody and the grouse would lose their habitat simply because the money from the "rich gunmen" was no longer available. It is easy to stand on a soap box and demand that shooting be stopped and that the maintenance money be found from "other sources". Finding those other sources is not quite as easy as it sounds.

The characters in this book are therefore sporting characters. They are hunters, shooters, fishers and gatherers of Nature's bounties. It is hard to explain to or try to convince those opposed that there *is* a strange kind of love between hunters and their quarry. I would hazard that most hunters, for instance, would vote against the keeping of mink or polecat ferrets in cages for their fur. Yet they are wise enough to know that releasing them into the wild (as has been done by mindless idiots in the past) hardly helps their cause. The vast majority of 1,000 or so mink, released illegally some years ago, died within the first week. The remaining survivors played havoc in poultry and fish farms and later gave the local Mink Hunt its best ever season!

I would hazard too that the characters portrayed here would, without exception, respect the views of those genuinely opposed to killing animals or the eating of meat. They would not agree with them but they would see them as honourable people and debate with them with dignity.

Some of the characters depicted will be recognised by the reader as poachers of a low order. Such men experienced hard times between the two world wars and later, when meat was rationed almost into non-existence, their fieldcraft produced food which would not otherwise have been available for their growing families.

The rich never suffered from the effects of rationing. Food of all kinds was always available at a price. The poor never had the price and so they went without many essentials. The poachers, who knew the score, saw no sin in gathering food for their families in any way possible. If the rich could break the law by buying on the black market, so too could the poor by using their outdoor skills.

When I was released from the armed forces at the end of the war, I used many of the old skills I had inherited from my father and uncles (who were honourable men but poachers nonetheless) and joined in the never-ending hunt for food.

There was a strange thrill about night-time poaching. A thrill that left a feeling of terror in my guts on every venture. I controlled it and I came back more often than not with the bounty but I doubt if I could ever claim to have enjoyed it. The joy came, no doubt, from the regular provision of food for the table, the sight of my young daughter and my immediate family relishing in the food I had provided *and* the occasional bonanza harvest which I was able to share with those less fortunate. I can say, with truth, that I could have sold my harvests to wealthy folk for a lot more hard cash but I never did. They had their own sources. I had my own outlets and my returns often came in the shape of a bag of sprouts, a bunch of carrots, a lettuce or a picking of broad beans!

I gave up the doubtful side of field sports when opportunities to shoot and fish came my way largely as a result of my eagerness to participate. Later, when my thoughts found their way into various journals, I met others with similar views and as a result of my scribblings, I developed an urge to travel.

Those travels brought me into contact with many other field sportsmen and took me to all corners of the globe. I have called a halt to them many times but inevitably, after a while, my feet begin to itch and I feel obliged to pack my sack and roll up my sleeping bag yet again.

Mine has been an interesting life and it has brought me into contact with many interesting sporting characters.

This book has ended up as a miscellany, a cavalcade or, if you prefer it, a lucky dip. It has ended up that way because I have found no chronological way of presenting it chapter by chapter. Nor, if I tell the truth, have I discovered a serious way of deciding "That's enough! No more"! That's what I ought to have done a long time ago, but I find it hard to leave out – say – Willy – because I have already included Wally!

All the characters included have been of great interest to

me. Many others, not mentioned, deserve a longer chapter of their own. How, for example, can I discuss the late Dick Walker (a wonderful friend, colleague, adviser and mentor) in one short chapter when I have written twelve or so long articles about him for the angling press. Those articles could have made a book (with a little licence) and I have not enough space to do the great man justice. The same applies to Peter Thomas, Chris Tarrant, Maurice Ingham, Fred Buller, Les Moncrieff, Malcolm Baldwin, Alec Martin and others too numerous to be mentioned here. And – what about the ladies? Have I not met, over the years, enough ladies to warrant a book in their own right? I am far from being a male chauvinist and I simply have to beg those ladies, both here and abroad, to forgive me for their exclusion!

There are, nevertheless, some very special friends and colleagues to whom I owe a debt of thanks. Where to start?

I have no doubts in my mind that Tony Jackson, one-time Editor of *Shooting Times* magazine, heads the list. I was well established as a writer on angling subjects when he paid me the compliment of commissioning a weekly article for his popular magazine. It was 1973. His proposal was that I should write a regular column under the title of "The Countryman". There *was* a mild hiccup for a year or so after Tony left the publication, but I am *still* writing a regular Countryman column. Tony had confidence in me. I feel I responded correctly and it is true to say that, either way, Tony and I have remained friends. I owe him a great deal!

I also owe a debt of gratitude to Paul Bach, Editor of *Saga* magazine, who, remembering my earlier writings as a coarse fish angler, paid me the compliment, eventually, of commissioning a monthly column for his famous magazine *SAGA Monthly*.

I take pride in the fact that I have written for *Saga* for almost ten years, and I thank Paul Bach for letting me include parts of my regular column in this book. It goes without saying that my association with Tim Paisley, Editor of *Carp World* magazine, has been one of sheer joy. Tim has given me the privilege of writing for his lovely publication as and when it suits me to do so. "You write it, I'll print it!" That was his offer to me over twelve years ago when he produced the very first issue. I am proud to have been associated, on a very frequent though not strictly regular basis, with what I regard as Britain's leading angling magazine, and I am grateful to Tim for letting me include earlier extracts in this book.

My problem is now magnified since I recognise that I could spend the rest of my life recording experiences with friends, colleagues, acquaintances and other lovers of the country-side. Space forbids me to include them; love and fellowship insists that I do!

Time flies! Deadlines have to be met. Will my readers accept some brief anecdotes regarding those I hold in high esteem and, perhaps, at some later date, look forward to reading full accounts of their association? Another book? Mine has been a long life. It has been enhanced by the cama-raderie of an incredible number of field sportsmen and lovers of the countryside. They ought to be included here even if only in anecdotal form. I hope they will forgive me if they are *not*! As a peace-offering, however, I will try to remind them here of our friendship *and* reassure them that its survival is guaranteed! The short, inter-chapter, links in the following pages represent my attempts at realising this hope and, with that hope in my heart, I leave it to my readers to decide.

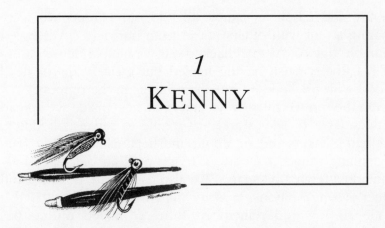

1
KENNY

I first saw Kenny wending his way across the road that separated Hartwell Pits from Hartwell Lake close to Aylesbury. He had a fishing rod in one hand and a landing net across his shoulder. In the landing net was an eel weighing 3lb and, having just acquired a beat-up rod and reel along with an urge to go fishing myself, I was fascinated. A childhood friendship began there and then which lasted until Kenny's death in 1989 – about 58 years later.

We were both at school – different schools – but we had bicycles and we loved the outdoors. Water attracted us and we spent our summers swimming, fishing, camping and "surviving" along the banks of the River Thame. Survival was not difficult. We could shoot as many small rabbits as we needed. We could catch eels, perch and crayfish from the river and when we were ordered home for a change of clothing, our parents replenished our supplies. We ran wild and loved every minute of our outdoor existence with the other local kids and we were hardly aware of the adults who obviously cared and watched us from a distance. We seldom saw them but there was always one there quickly in an emergency. We enjoyed a freedom which most parents today would not dare to bestow upon their children. On the other hand, of course, most of today's youngsters prefer to watch TV or soccer. It is their privilege.

Deep in the wooded banks and well off the beaten track,

Kenny and I built a camp. We told our parents we were sharing a tent with others but in truth our only cover was a bramble "igloo". We had hacked our way into a dense clump of blackberry bush having hauled out great heaps of dead wood with pricked and bleeding fingers in the process.

On the top we piled twigs and branches. Inside we spread a thick layer of leaves and leaf mould to serve as bedding. We had blankets and an old groundsheet, fishing tackle, bait, swimming trunks, matches, a frying pan, an old black billy can and a few rabbit snares. We also had bread, potatoes and other assorted rations. It never rained in those days! Had it done so I would remember! It never rained during our childhood. Ask any grandparent and he will confirm that statement!

That igloo camp was our secret. We spent time in tents and shared campfires with other village kids but Kenny and I hunted rabbits, caught fish and spent hours on end swimming in the river using the igloo as base. Our clothes, such as they were, became disgustingly filthy but we spent too much time in the water ever to become dirty ourselves. We each carried a catapult and spent much time each day scratching around for pebbles or "dabbers". We also spent time practising our skills shooting at baked bean tins suspended on a string. And just once in a while we would pick off a young rabbit in the cool of the evening and hang it inside the igloo out of reach of the creatures of the night.

By today's standards, of course, our bird's egg hunting activities were unlawful but I can say, hand on heart, that we never caused any bird to desert her nest. We took an egg here and there for collections but we never truly robbed nests. Even those most prized of all eggs, those of the moorhen, were never over-exploited. On our long swims in the river (often several miles at a stretch, taking into consideration the tough upstream pull and the relaxed downstream drift) we searched for and encountered many nests. We tested the eggs to see how far developed they were and left those too far gone for use as food. From others we took a couple here and a couple there, always paying return visits to take note of and purloining any seen to be extra to those we had left previously. Kenny fashioned a scoop with a dessertspoon whipped to a willow stick for stealing eggs we could not reach when on our bankside walks.

We gathered mushrooms in abundance and cooked them with the eggs for breakfast or supper depending upon the state of our larder.

We followed the country code in terms of farm gates and we took the trouble to report incidents of sheep or cattle in any kind of trouble. It is fair to say that we earned the respect of some local farmers and that despite our youth we learned to be responsible.

Kenny and I grew up together. We were two of a kind and we both had a wanderlust.

He went into the Merchant Navy and I went into the Royal Tank Corps (later to become the Royal Tank Regiment) simply to satisfy a desire to see other parts of the world. We lost track of each other then but renewed our friendship at the end of hostilities.

I took up fishing seriously again. Kenny merely dabbled. He became an adept magician and eventually made a good living pulling rabbits out of hats and other strange places.

He still loved the outdoors and enjoyed fishing and hunting rabbits, hare, pheasant, wild duck or whatever other quarry presented itself. His favourite saying regarding wild duck was to the effect that "If you have duck for dinner you only need two at the table. You and the duck!" A sentiment with which many would perhaps agree!

Wanderlust hit me before Kenny's feet began to itch again. I began spending time in the USA. He developed a true love for Cornwall and eventually bought a guest house there to live in semi-retirement. My wife and I became regular visitors and I spent much time with Kenny negotiating cliff descents in order to fish off the rocks for pollack, plaice, mackerel or whatever else happened to be available.

Kenny was not a tall man but he was a big man. Very much overweight at 18 stone, he became red-faced and short of breath climbing back up those cliffs and yet he was as light and sure-footed as a cat. There were special tracks up and down which he had learned over the years and he followed them confidently. A handhold here, a foothold there, a wriggle around an outcrop or a leap across a void between rocks were all part of his daily fishing ventures.

If I said I was not scared I would be lying but I felt obliged to tackle anything Kenny undertook. I had always been able to in the past. I was nevertheless glad to get down to any chosen spot and overjoyed to get back up again.

"This is no joke," I remarked during one particularly hazardous descent. "It's a long way down."

"Ah," replied Kenny. "Think how it'd be trying to climb *up* from the bottom on a paint ladder. Watch this bit; it's as greasy as a butcher's navel."

When he was not fishing, he was either beachcombing or gardening. He was good at both. His home was enhanced with wooden beams, carved models and ornaments all of which originated as "finds" on one or other of the many Lizard beaches. How he managed to haul up some of the bigger items of flotsam defies description but he always insisted that he "took it in small doses".

When beer went up to 25 pence per pint Kenny jibbed.

"I refuse to pay five bob for a pint of ale," he said. "That's the last the pub will see of me."

And he started brewing his own bitter beer a few days later. He studied the subject well and finally mastered the process starting from the basic grain and other ingredients. He soon developed a regular production routine and produced at least 40 pints of excellent ale every week for many years. It was not strong ale but very refreshing. He would come in from his garden or allotment and quaff a couple of pints before going back to his labours.

"Beer should be enjoyed as a drink and not taken for its alcohol effect," he assured me. "Anyone can make strong beer, but who wants to drink a pint and fall over?"

He added that the main reason for his hard work in the garden was to work up a thirst and enjoy his beer. There was a lot more to it than that, of course.

He grew enough vegetables for himself and his guests every year. For the most part his wife Miriam served freshly gathered garden produce daily. Such was their reputation for fine fare that neither she nor Kenny were obliged to advertise their holiday service. Fresh fish, crab, lobster and other sea food were part of the whole economy. Fresh farm beef, lamb, pork, bacon and eggs were accepted as wages for work done. Kenny would crew for a small boat skipper, paint a new sign for a restaurant or repoint a brick chimney in return for a supply of fresh produce. What he could not use at once was stored in freezers for his own use when the holiday season was over. He gave the best to his guests and welcomed the same ones each year but he was always glad when the happy holiday-makers left and the village was quiet once more.

"I wish they'd stay away and just send their money," he would say when the luxury coaches arrived each day. He would then pick up his daily newspaper, retire to his spare garage-cum-wine cellar-cum-brewery and await the arrival of his local friends. These were mostly gardening or fishing associates but they included local odd job men and others.

They all had a taste for Kenny's beer which is why he occasionally had to put down a reserve 40-pint brew. He was generous with his beer and knew full well that those who enjoyed it were always on call for help with a particular problem. Besides which, of course, as he assured me so many times, his beer cost all-in about 7 pence per pint when that in the pub cost in the region of one pound sterling!

Since those days, although not a beer drinker myself, I keep a few litres of my own home brew for friends who are!

It was during one of those midday sessions in the garage that the prevailing drought conditions were being discussed and in particular the potato crop generally. All it seemed were suffering.

"How are yours turning out?" asked Lofty. Kenny put his hand in his old jacket and pulled out five potatoes about the size of cherries.

"There's a sample," he said. "All the rest are little 'uns. And if anyone fancies them 'mangy-toot peas' they might as well pick all my main crop. They're never going to fill out now!"

His sense of humour never left him and his garden stories were a joy. He grew redcurrants for show one year and was very disappointed to receive only third prize for his efforts. He told us it was only later that he learned he had been given third prize for tomatoes!

He loved children. He did not particularly like those little know-alls who were always out to spoil his magic tricks. There were more than enough of those, he insisted, but once you recognised their existence it was easy to handle them. You must never patronise them but lead them on and make them laugh. Their parents were paying for your services!

He had no children of his own. That was a cross he had to bear through no fault of his own or of his wife. Children, however, loved him, his grey hair and sideburns and his permanent smile.

"You are a lucky man, Taylor," he told me once when my own granddaughter hugged him with affection. "Look at this. What wish could you better for?"

It was a favourite expression of his and we had both used it a million times since childhood instead of "what better could you wish for?"

"What wish could you better for?" he had said when we were kids baking potatoes in the campfire embers.

"What wish could you better for?" he had said as we sat in the sun on the Cornish rocks watching the guillemots in the distance.

"It's a nice way to go," he had said of an old mutual friend who had dozed off and died in his sleep. "What wish could you better for?"

Kenny never knew a day's really serious illness in his life, which he enjoyed to the full. I know, however, that he had a dread of a long and lingering lead up to the end when it came. As it happened, he too was stricken with a sudden heart attack so severe that he never regained consciousness. I was shocked and saddened but I knew it was how he would have chosen.

And given the opportunity at this very moment I am sure he would shrug his shoulders, grin and ask, "What wish could you better for?"

"Mutual Respect"

His name was Sykes and, of course, everyone called him Bill. He was a local character and his dealings in the Fylde district of Lancashire were not always strictly legitimate.

It was my practice, as a soldier recently sent home from France during the war, to cycle across Pilling Sands to Knott End, catch the ferry to Fleetwood and spend some time with my young wife. Often I called at an inn for a brief respite about half-way across the sands. I cannot remember the name of the inn but I remember that I always called it the "Half-way House".

I was very fit in those days but, even so, 18 miles of pedalling warranted, I thought, a pint of ale half-way. I made it a regular stop, winter and summer.

On one occasion there was, behind the bar, a brace of pheasants hung up in all their splendour. They had been brought in by Bill Sykes and the deal had been done.

It so happened, however, that the local bobby, new to the job, spotted them before the landlord had had time to put them out of sight.

He questioned their presence.

"Bill Sykes brought 'em in," said mine host. "They'd flown into t' telegraph wires."

The constable considered the situation.

"That's as may be," he said, "But thee tell Bill Sykes, if he happens across a good 'are that's hit t' telegraph wires, I'm in t' market for it!"

14

~-2
WILLIE

We travelled up to Glencaple casually on a Sunday. I had not been wildfowling since my early post-war years and this was to be a fresh, sporting and social occasion. Paul Goss and I were part of a party organised by Fred Buller who was then busy developing his "Chubbs of Edgeware" business. That was in 1964. We could not find the Nith Hotel. Glencaple on Sunday afternoon was just a sleepy village. There was no-one to ask.

After passing a smoke-stained ruin several times, we realised that this had to be the Nith Hotel. Or what remained of it!

"We've a wee bitty 'o' problem," said the proprietor Willie Houliston. " 'Naei Hotel!"

He went on to tell us the story. There had been a fire. The books had been burned. He had no addresses to contact us and cancel the arrangements. He had done his best. He would continue to do his best to accommodate us. And he did! We slept here, there and everywhere other than in proper beds – but I have to say it brought us all together.

Willie had commandeered the nearby village hall to serve as a bar room and it was there that I got to meet "Whisper" (he could NOT talk quietly), "Ron the Dog" (his dog tried to molest everyone sleeping on or near the floor!), "Lennie the Lion" (a placid young man with no aggression), "odds-on-Henry" (a part-time bookmaker) and many others given nicknames on the spot.

Paul became "Rapala", since he had lost a very expensive fishing lure first cast. It was *not his* lure to lose! "Michael the Gent" (a Midlands manufacturer whose perfect manners were to his eternal credit), "Lord Pacey" (simply because that is how his behaviour tended to present him), and Mr Cleaver, the finest storyteller of all time who became known as "George" because that *was* his name!

There were others, of course. I became "Fred-the-Fish". Fred Buller became "Fred-the-Gun". So it continued.

At about 3.00 a.m. we were practising judo in the village hall! At 4.30 a.m. we were opening champagne for no reason at all. And shortly afterwards we located our makeshift beds and decided to get a night's sleep!

At dawn it was a slightly different world that greeted us. "It seemed like a good idea at the time," said Whisper.

"How many birthdays did I celebrate?" asked Lennie. "What's happened to my dog?" asked Ron.

We ought to have known better but, somehow, we did not! This was our regular procedure for the next six nights.

I had not played a guitar for many years (and I never was much good anyway!) but someone produced a guitar and I became the "star turn". It does *NOT really bear thinking about* but such were those early days at the Nith. That is how the scene developed!

Each year more friends joined us. Each year the social side of it superseded the serious sporting aspects involved.

It went on for 21 years! Occasionally one or other of the group managed to harvest a goose, but it really mattered little. The progress of "The Pilgrims", as we began to call ourselves, was more important than quarry!

Eventually, as more and more of our numbers moved on (or passed on), our visits ceased and in many respects I am truly glad they did! What I could handle in the 1960s and 70s is somewhat different from what I can handle today! The pace has had to slow down considerably! At 80 plus years I cannot handle what I did at 45! But I have my memories and the one that stands out above all others is the remark made by Willie when I paid my final bill.

"Them's awfy expensive breakfasts, Fred," he said. "Ye have 'nae been to your bed all week!"

Happy days, but *PLEASE*, no more!

"Ruffled Feathers"

Nobby was out of work and he was going through a bad patch. It was Christmas, and he could not afford the customary goose, turkey, chicken (a luxury in those days!) or whatever. He had an allotment which was his pride and joy and, if Nobby had little else in the way of Christmas fare he, at least, had vegetables. Plenty of them – especially onions.

He was a proud man and it distressed him to be idle, but he put on a show during that particular holiday period which endeared him to his friends and totally confused his enemies.

In those days it was possible to buy suet for a few coppers from the local butcher and, since very few folk needed suet over the holiday, Nobby struck a deal. He could afford one substantial pork chop. It would feed him well on Christmas Day. That, and a chunk of suet, provided him with plenty of dripping (after rendering) and a visit to the local poulterer/game dealer/fishmongers provided him with several necks (turkey, goose, etc.) and a couple of handfuls of feathers (all retrieved from the dustbin area!).

Nobby, on Christmas morning, "decorated" his own dustbin with scattered feathers and discarded necks-and-heads.

As lunch-time approached, he opened his windows, put a basinful of chopped onions into the frying pan with a wedge of dripping, added a pinch of sage-and-thyme and let the pan sizzle.

He swore, until his dying day many years later, that those neighbours, passing to and from the local pub, eyed the feathers and heads, sniffed the aroma of frying onions and associated it all with a superb Christmas feast. Nobby's Christmas lunch was well advertised!

On the face of it, who could argue?

Is there any more appetizing smell than a pan of cooking onions-and-herbs? And if the locals were fooled, is it any big deal? Perhaps a little pride of this nature is to be recommended and admired in these modern days of "full and plenty".

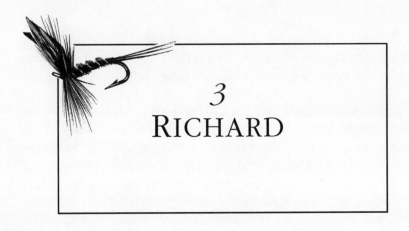

3
RICHARD

There is no doubt about the fact that Richard Walker and all he represented should be featured exclusively in a book bearing that title. It is possible that someone, some day, will write it but, in the meantime, it is essential that he becomes part of this one. I knew him as Dick because he preferred it that way. He was Richard to colleagues, he said, but always Dick to his friends.

He died at 3.00 a.m. on August 2nd 1985 and left the world of angling with an emptiness which, I venture to say, will never be filled again. For over 30 years we were as close as two friends could ever be and, although we had rarely fished together during the last several years of his life, we each knew we could rely upon the other if need be. Even now I find it hard to write this chapter.

It would be easy for me to become sentimental, for I am a somewhat sentimental person, and yet I know that Dick would not wish me to be so. He was always a practical man and his scientific approach to all problems left little room for pathos. He was, however, a kind and thoughtful person, generous to a fault and always ready to lend a helping hand to those less fortunate. The late Jimmy James, who made and marketed his original Mark IV carp rod, referred to him as "a kind, generous and dignified man whose air of arrogance was utterly contrived". He probably came about as near to understanding Dick Walker as anyone could, since their relationship had to do with practicalities. I could not put a better description on an old friend than that offered by Jimmy James in those heydays of built cane, balanced paste and goose quills. Dick once referred to my brother, my cousin and me as a "joyous crew" and I have to say that it was a fair description. I also have to say that the last time I saw Dick was a joyous occasion. He was seriously ill then, but such was his extrovert nature that he refused to allow any mention of it. As Peter Thomas (his dearest friend who was with him almost to the end), Fred Buller and I sat down to the last meal we had together, he declared that he was going to enjoy being in company with "the three men I like most in this world". Then, without any sign of embarrassment, he made a hasty correct. "I should have said the three men I *love* most," he announced. Somewhere, there was a wealth of tenderness in his make-up and sometimes he allowed it to show!

Our friendship came about in an odd way and yet I am in no doubt that it was destined to be. We who followed Dick's exploits, and read his column in various journals, were of the same spawn but with less courage of our own convictions. We looked up to him and read him avidly because we saw in him what we ourselves would like to be and, when his revolutionary book *Still-Water Angling* was published in 1953, it was like a gentle fall of rain in the desert. Here was someone who fished lakes and ponds and reservoirs and who knew their potential as we did. It was the first of its kind ever to be devoted to fishing in waters with no flow, and we grasped it eagerly.

I could not regard what I read of tench fishing in it as erroneous but I felt it was incomplete and wrote a letter to him to say so. My wife was furious. "How dare you write to disagree with an expert?" she demanded. I was apprehensive myself but what I had to say had to be said!

A week or so later a letter from Dick Walker put my mind at rest. He saw my point, asked my opinion on another matter, and a friendship began to mature. The following summer we entertained Dick and Peter Thomas on our boat at Wotton Lakes and, if there was any convincing needed, we convinced them both that we had done our homework regarding tench fishing. I had, meanwhile, written an article on spec for the old *Angler's News* which was, at that time, edited by one Peter Whittaker and, to my delight, it was accepted and printed in that journal.

That one effort would have been my one and only venture into journalism had it not been for Dick Walker who not only encouraged but literally bullied me into writing more!

He turned up one day with a small 35mm camera which he presented me with, saying that he had bought it cheaply as a job lot. I could repay him, he said, out of the money I would earn from journalism in due course. I was horrified since I had never owed anyone a single penny until then. I still do not know whether I paid full price for that camera! Dick Walker could lie like a trooper to save someone less fortunate any embarrassment, and I still have a feeling that he did so on that occasion! I did, however, realise that I had to earn the money to pay for it and, as a result, launched myself into a career of part-time journalism.

In the many years that followed I have, as a result of his influence, followed that career with reasonable success and I know that my life and my lifestyle changed from the day I first met him.

It was said by many that he was too engrossed in the pursuit of big fish. That he was incapable of appreciating the dawns and the sunsets, the bird chorus or the smell of water-mint. The beauties of nature, they said, were beyond his ken, as was his ability to enjoy a joke. If only they had known!

It would take a library of books to record the hilarious tales of exploits of Dick Walker and his own joyous crew of stal-warts. Despite the seriousness of their approach to fishing, they would never lose sight of the fact that fishing was to be enjoyed. And in that respect the disciples emulated their master. He wrote, in the preface of his now classic book, that there would always be those ready to point out that there is much more to fishing than catching fish. That the charm of angling lies in the escape it provides from everyday life, the beauty of its surroundings and the wildlife of the waterside. Dick Walker was at pains to point out that success in catch-ing fish did not render a man oblivious to those things and that failure to write about them did not mean that he failed to recognise their values. A man is not an atheist, he said, simply because he does not bawl about his faith in the street. Those who professed to scorn the mere catching of fish were, he said, really very anxious to catch them. They were desolated when a big one broke off and escaped!

It was nigh impossible to fault Dick's logic and it was said by many that to argue with him in print was the height of folly. They were almost invariably right, since he had the politician's flair for debate. He would always say, however, that the object of an argument was to arrive at the truth and not specifically to win at all costs. He seldom lost an argument but when he did he accepted it graciously and emphasised that it had served to bring truth to the fore. I hardly ever argued with him for the simple reason that I knew I could never win. He deliberately went out of his way to win arguments with those closest to him but it was noticeable to us all that he often used our own trains of thought in later debates. He knew that we would forgive him for deliberately confusing us with his pseudo logic but he never used it against those who were not wise to his wiles. That would have been a mismatch, and he knew it!

I could tell of hilarious weekends with him and other members of the Carp Catcher's Club. I could tell of serious ventures into the world of what is now known as "specimen hunting". I could tell of the lies we both told, not to achieve anything in the way of recognition, but rather to deflate someone's rather pompous ego. Dick Walker was like that and I needed no encouragement to follow suit. I could tell of big fish hooked and lost. I could tell of frustrating blanks, and I could tell of weekend camps when fishing revolved only around our ability to catch perch, grayling, trout, eels, pike, gudgeon or crayfish to supplement our rations. As we mellowed in our approach, we began to appreciate that there was indeed more to fishing than catching fish!

I will tell instead the tale of Joe Taylor's 26lb carp, as reported by Dick Walker at the time.

"Most of the carp were rolling about in the weeds but Joe noticed a fish swimming up and down at the dam end and decided to try a floating crust bait. After inspecting it several times the carp took the bait and was hooked. It bolted through the weeds and emerged in a narrow strip of water between the weed bed and the bank. There it stuck. Joe was on one side of the weed bed, the carp on the other, and neither able to do much about it. Fred solved the problem by wading out with a long-handled net. The first few steps took him to his knees, the next few to his waist. He looked round to us on the dam and said, 'That's funny, the water only came two inches up them ducks!'"

I don't remember saying it and I doubt very much if I did, but it doesn't matter. It enhanced the story of a big fish caught in all seriousness by a group of anglers totally dedicated to the capture of specimens. It recorded the capture without losing the atmosphere of what proved to be a joyous occasion. That is what Dick Walker was all about. That is how

I will remember him. I am but one of many thousands who will miss his great qualities and I still grieve that he is no longer with us.

4
RON

Back in 1977, I found myself in Western Australia for the first time. I had my fishing rod with me but there seemed to be no place to fish other than the ocean, which was close by. I had gone to see my daughter and my granddaughter.

Since then, and after a dozen or so visits, I have learned a little about the wildlife, the people and the terrain. I am still likely to get lost in the bush but I see an improvement in my sense of direction. Which is comforting. All those years ago I was looking for somewhere to fish that did not involve putting out to sea and becoming violently seasick. I wanted to cast from a river or lake bank and, if possible, sit under a tree and watch a float. If I should nod it into oblivion I was not too concerned. Float fishing can be like that at times and is, perhaps, all the better for it.

Over a glass of Australian nondescript lager in the tavern one evening, I heard tell of a small, secluded lake, only a mile or so away but in the bush and off the beaten track. My informant, an ex-Liverpudlian, assured me that there were perch aplenty to be caught, and advised me regarding bait, method and direction. I located the lake after negotiating many rusty, barbed wire fences and other obstacles. On the way, I encountered a few sheep, an aggressive ram, several geese, a fat pig, two horses and three goats. It occurred to me at once that I was on private property and that the small lake was not there for anyone to fish without permission! And not wishing to be at fault, I set to work with my son-in-law, Ian Howcroft, an Australian resident, to locate the owner. He turned out to be one Ron Hoffner who was, in my opinion, a true bushman, despite having a magnificent home in Perth city. I knew at a glance that he was happy in jeans and bush boots, that he could curl up and sleep anywhere, at anytime, and that he preferred the shelter of the big gum trees to an air-conditioned flat in the city.

He looked at us strangely when we asked if we might fish the lake. He gave us permission readily but assured us that there were no fish of any kind to be caught. We tried and, in due course, felt obliged to agree with him.

It was, however, the start of a friendship that never wavered for an instant during the years that followed.

In a way, Ron and I were, and still are, two of a kind. We both love the great outdoors, we both love to hunt game in the widest sense for the pot, and we are both agreed that it is sinful to kill game or whatever without good reason. Most of our quarry is eaten but since foxes kill his chickens and my pheasants, they are included on both our "wanted" lists.

In the normal course of a day in the bush, Ron, a superb horseman, will ride one of his many mounts to locate spots where rabbits are available. I have been fortunate enough to ride one of his soft old steeds myself (though I am no horse-man) to prove that rabbits, kangaroos and other forms of life in the bush are not intimidated by a mounted rider. I have known Ron shoot many a rabbit for supper from one of his perfectly steady horses.

He and I have had an agreement for years and I cannot fault it. "Bring the onions and, if you like, some flour for the damper," he orders. "I'll bring the wine and the rifle, and we'll sack-out afterwards under the gum trees and feel sorry for the city folk!"

I have never known it to fail. One or other of us has always managed to get a supper rabbit and, under the strange but fascinating stars of the southern sky, we have eaten of succulent meat and crusty hot bread smoothed on its way with superb Australian wine. Simple fare but with added ingredients that beggar description. Night skies, the sweet scent of the bush, campfire smoke, billy tea and an appetite that defies all. There is no better way to go.

During our years of friendship, Ron and I have lain in wait overnight for foxes after cooking rabbits on sticks on an open fire. We have stalked emus and kangaroos, without intent to kill. We have indulged in crayfish "cookouts" and we have feasted on other wild and readily available game. I well remember one night over the New Year's holiday period many years ago when, along with an old and respected Aussie friend, Ernie Chitty, we shot and dressed out a kangaroo, casseroled (laugh if you wish – it doesn't bother me!) several pigeon, half a dozen parrots (legal then) and a brace of rabbits to eat before sliding into the comfort of our sleeping bags under the eucalyptus trees. The scent of the gum trees is alien to anything we enjoy in the UK but I hold it special because I have learned to accept and respect the bushland's harsh and unyielding environment.

Today in the pleasant warmth of the Australian early evening sun, I am able to relate to the differences between our outdoor worlds. In the shade of a magnificent blackboy tree (its dry, upper foliage has formed the basis of many campfires) I recall the mosquitoes that drove me almost crazy until the fire was dampened to produce smoke. I remember how the old truck had been bogged in the sand when we tried to negotiate a fallen timber obstacle. I remember shooting at (and missing) a prime early-evening rabbit target. I remember Ron showing me the horrendous ticks on a goanna or bob-tailed lizard. He spent a great deal of time picking off those ticks that were lodged between the scales on the wretched creatures body. He had, and still has, the patience of Job. He also has a soft heart and feelings for the lesser creatures of the bush. He will kill without hesitation for food and to protect his livestock but any injured creature may look to him for help and be sure to receive it.

This kind of attitude, as I see it, puts Ron on par with 99 per cent of British field sportsmen! We are a strange lot indeed. We set out to kill, by whatever means, a wild creature that we see as quarry. Should we, en route, stumble across – say – an injured leveret, however, most of us would have second thoughts about its end. In its prime it is fair game but when seen to be at a disadvantage it needs help and true sporting help is invariably forthcoming.

Field sportsmen, it seems, are the same the whole world over. It is to their credit but not easy for those opposed to understand!

There is an old, ramshackle cabin deep in the bush that is Ron's property. It is presently suffering from the attacks of termites but the roof is sound and the old table where we have shared many a breakfast, lunch and supper is still intact. A million ants march back and forth between its gum-wood legs and exploit the banksia cones on the surrounding sand. The sand is grey, since it has, over many years, mingled with the charcoal following monstrous bush fires. It covers a person with dirt that is not strictly dirty! Hard to understand but even more difficult to explain to the lady of the house who has to handle the laundry on one's return!

At that table, over many years, Ron and I have exchanged confidences, eaten kangaroo steaks, popped the corks from many bottles of Aussie champagne, taunted kookaburras, told lies, eaten freshly picked figs, endured the dry heat of Western Australia, and cemented a friendship that sets more solidly as the years pass. We have drunk gallons of billy tea – black as night and hot as fire – from tin cans, enamel mugs and discarded jam jars. And we have sat and listened to the kindly voices of the bush creatures in the daylight and the darkness.

Used plates, cups and other utensils require washing up after use but water is always precious. There is no real shortage but hauling containers in the bush by hand makes one appreciate its value. Ron's answer to that problem is simple. He lays a thin trail of honey (wild bees produce it for those brave enough to harvest it) from floor to table and leaves the ants to take care of the crocks! Next morning a wipe with a disinfectant cloth sees the pots and pans "squeaky clean". Ants can be bothersome at times but they have their uses in the bush! They thrive in their billions and yet it is hard to figure out how they manage it. In the main, the Australian bush is sterile, dry and devoid of the compost that encourages organic life. Somehow or other, however, the ants survive and reproduce. Their natural enemies are few and yet there is one fierce assailant that remains, for the most part, unseen and unsuspected. Ron refers to it as the "ant-lion" and has demonstrated to me many times how this minute ambusher handles its quarry.

I have no idea what an ant-lion looks like but Ron apparently does. And, because he knows exactly what he is looking for, he is able to direct a lone ant to its doom by drawing a line in the sand (with a fingertip) towards a hidden ant-lion. The unsuspecting ant proceeds until, in about one-millionth of a heartbeat, it is seized from cover and devoured. I have watched it happen many times but I still cannot come to terms with the amazing speed of it all. It really has to be seen to be believed! That, however, could apply to countless other aspects of the bush! My only regret is that my time spent in that particular environment has always been, and unfortunately will always be, limited. I have served but half an apprenticeship! I am unlikely ever to graduate but I have found great pleasure in my simple quest.

It is doubtful if I will ever come to terms with serious ferreting in temperatures of 100°F plus. Or with shooting rabbits in the infra-red spotlight beam when dressed only in shorts and slippers. Such sporting exercises are, without doubt, easier to endure than our own wintertime hunts in temperatures well below freezing. But summer out here is the one time when rabbits do not breed. Water is short, grass is dry and doe rabbits can produce little or no milk in the circumstances. Walking around with a shotgun, however, is not quite as pleasurable as it is in the United Kingdom.

It takes a deal of getting used to and rabbits shot in these conditions have to be dressed out quickly. Ice boxes have to be carried for that purpose and, while it is easy to make unfavourable comparisons between our own winter rabbits and those in the bush, there is a sweetness to the flesh of the

31

flea-ridden wretches of Western Australia that puts them in a class of their own.

Ron is convinced that mosquito bites produce less swelling and discomfort if the creature is left to take its ration of blood uninterrupted. He insists that people who swipe at a biting insect do themselves more harm. The mosquito, he says, injects a fluid into the human's blood in order to dilute it and make it acceptable. This fluid contains a poison which, in fact, causes the actual swelling. If the bite is not interrupted, most of the poison is withdrawn along with the blood. Since he never appears to be affected one way or the other (he never swipes at mosquitoes and he never suffers from bites) I can only assume that there is some truth in his theory.

On reflection, the only other person I knew who appeared to be totally immune to bites was the late Ted Trueblood of Idaho. I never heard him make the same claim but I have watched him study monstrous Rocky Mountain mosquitoes enjoying a drink at his expense. He would sometimes remark that "This little sucker's having a good time" or words to that effect. He never, to my knowledge, did anything to deter them. He, too, was a truly incredible bushman. He had a great deal in common with Ron Hoffner and I truly wish they might have met sometime. Alas, it can never be!

The small lake on Ron's property appeared to both of us to offer an opportunity for crayfish stocking. There are, as far as I know, four kinds of freshwater crayfish in Australia. Yabbies are small, tasty but somewhat labour-intensive. Gilgies and cunacks are larger and might be compared, in size, to the American signal crayfish now firmly established in British waters after the virtual demise of our own natives. I can never tell the difference between gilgies and cunacks. The Australian marron is by far the largest of the freshwater crays. It is the lobster of creek, dam or pond and is subject to a season and a bag limit.

I harvested a larger cooler box of gilgies at one time and transported them 150 miles to stock Ron's pond. I lost a few but the majority survived and multiplied.

The lake dried up completely the following summer,

however, and shags, which appeared from nowhere, cleared them out by the thousand. In two years the population had exploded and our harvest hopes were high for the following year. On reflection, perhaps we should have exploited stocks earlier!

There is a swamp quite close to Ron's pond, however, that never dries completely. It is green and shady and rabbits love the surrounding short, green grass. It is a superb place for a campfire and an overnight stay, and both Ron and I decided it would be a good spot to plant new stocks. The water is shallow but obviously cooler and more protected from marauding birds since it has a natural "roof" of trees, shrubs and vines.

I saved a bucketful of cunacks from a distant haul on my last visit to South-West Australia, and introduced them to the swamp after an overnight sojourn in the refrigerator. The latest news from Ron is that they appear to have survived and will soon be ready to harvest.

I hope so. There is no edible fish, fowl or game in my book that can hold a candle to freshly caught cunacks. I have tried many forms of wild food (more than most, I'd dare bet) but cunacks have me drooling at the thought.

Nor is there any better place in the world to prepare and eat them than in Ron's little corner of the bush. I have a feeling that there is a treat in store for us when, God willing, I next return. If and when it so happens, I know there will be a welcome for me at "Ron's Ranch". And he knows that, after family niceties have been completed, it will be my first port of call!

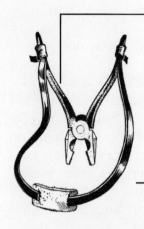

5
DISMAL

He was playing with a whip and top when I first met him and, although I do not strictly remember the last time I saw him, it is probably safe to say that he was drinking a pint of ale! Desmond, or Dismal as he preferred to call himself, loved a pint of English bitter. So much so that he very often chose to drink one!

As kids we roamed what was referred to as "The Common" in search of birds' eggs. We climbed trees, dammed up the Pebble Brook to make it deep enough for swimming, and generally lived an outdoor life whenever possible.

Later we both took to fishing, shooting and working ferrets. When we met again, after the war, we continued to hunt for any wild food that was available to us. We were both married and proud fathers of one child each. Rationing was strict, food was in short supply, and we felt a need to provide more. We, therefore, bent the rules a little from time to time. Early morning jaunts on bicycles with single-barrelled shotguns strapped to the crossbars were common occurrences. Seasons were honoured; boundaries were not! Here and there we had permission to shoot rabbits but I confess now that we were inclined to overstep our territories from time to time. We were also very guilty of taking game without proper licences. Pheasants were rare in those days. They were made even rarer when they came within our range. There was nothing nice about our "sporting" activities. We were pot-hunters and birds were not encouraged to fly before they were shot.

The standing joke between us was "You're surely not going to shoot that pheasant while it's running?"

"Of course not. I'm waiting until it stops!"

Partridges in those days, unlike today's paranoid specimens, often flushed a few feet ahead of us and we never hesitated to blast off into the covey. Nothing was sacred, other than the recognised seasons. We were never guilty of exploitation. With, perhaps, one exception. We took advantage of the "mad" hares during March.

We called them to us by "squawking" (sucking hard on a finger to produce the sound of a distressed doe) and shot them where they sat. Almost invariably the calls were answered by jack hares seeking mates and we looked upon each one as several pounds of red meat in a meat-hungry world!

There were no freezers in those days and refrigerators were few and far between. We never shot more hares than two (in total) and we often split one down the middle between us. Even a single hare becomes less appetizing after the third serving! We had no other choice. The hare had been killed and so it had to be eaten.

Rabbits were our main quarry, however, and we were not bothered much, one way or the other, how we acquired them. It is true we could only eat one at a time but we were encouraged to kill as many as we could by any means at our disposal. We knew a friendly butcher who would take our surplus for cash or in exchange for meat and offal. We took the latter option simply because we could then spread out our meat supplies. The deals were done. So many rabbits represented a chunk of liver today, a pound of good sausages mid-week and perhaps a small joint at the weekend. The pleasing part about it all was that the butcher did not care for shot rabbits and since we were always short of cartridges, we were happy to hunt them by other means.

The deadliest method of harvesting rabbits is with the use of strategically placed snares, and an opportunity to spend a night in "uncharted territory" came our way on one occasion. A certain farmer had left for a weekend in Devon, and Dismal and I set over a hundred snares on the hill that overlooked his house. We were safe. The house was empty and there was a big barn close by where we hung our quarry. As dawn approached, we picked up the remaining snares, gutted the rabbits and prepared to haul them over to our cycles. There were 49 in all.

My stomach turned over as the light in the farmhouse came on and Dismal whispered "He's back early!"

It was not a happy situation. Here we were in the farmer's barn with 49 of his rabbits hanging up around us. Should he decide to look around (and what was to stop him?) we were in trouble.

Dismal said, "We'll have to wait it out." And we did just that. After what seemed hours the bedroom lights came on and the downstairs lights were extinguished. A few moments later the house was in darkness. We strung the rabbits, gathered up the snares and made for home. Riding a bicycle with 25 rabbits hanging from all points is not easy. Our first mile was all downhill and positively dangerous but we made it, laughing our heads off all the way.

It seems almost impossible to believe that all that happened over 40 years ago and that I still have a few dozens of those very snares left. They cost just over half a penny each (in today's currency) and are still used to catch the occasional coney for the pot.

Dismal was an expert driver of cars and lorries. He drove big articulated vehicles with ease and confidence and knew his way around London as well as many other big cities. He always wanted to be rich and made many plans to coin a fortune but he never made it. In the process he made quite a lot of money here and there but he never really gave thought to investment. He became, as a result of study and experience, an expert on earthworms or "lobworms" as they are called in the fishing tackle industry.

On a mild, rainy night he would dress up in waterproofs and, wearing kneepads, collect from sports fields and short grass verges as many as 4,000 worms before dawn. It was hard work but extremely profitable since every tackle dealer in London was eager to buy all he had to spare.

He would phone me as soon as he knew I was awake and ask if I was going to London. Almost invariably I was. If not, I would change my schedule to suit him. I could always find business in London's tackle shops since I represented Messrs F. Goddard at the time. I knew that Dismal would drive my car, despite having been awake all night and that I could count on calling up at least half a dozen of my best customers that day. They were pleased to see us both.

Four thousand lobworms represented about two weeks' average wages in those days and since Dismal collected cash at all times, he should have been very well off for a number of years. Somehow, however, the holes in his pockets grew in proportion to their contents. A few pints here, a bet on the gee-gees there, and soon the surplus was gone.

He saved enough once to join me on a trip to Arkansas where he made a host of new friends. During his two-week stay he became very ill with some kind of infection that caused his face to swell grotesquely. The American doctor who treated him opted to "give him a shot" and the very mention of the words caused his condition to worsen. Dismal had a horror of needles! He was never ashamed to admit it. His spell in the forces had been injection-free because he had refused them all at all times. No-one, he declared, would ever stick needles into his flesh. He would rot in jail first!

Over in the USA he was obliged to change his mind – or have it changed for him. Details are somewhat vague and no-one seems really sure whether he passed out before or after the needle was introduced! He was, however, soon on the mend and out catching fish with some of the finest guides in Arkansas.

We threw a party for the locals of Rogers Town on the night before we left. It was our opportunity to say "thank you" to all the marvellous people who had entertained us so lavishly during our stay. Dismal insisted upon referring to American beer as "sodee-pop" and was determined to prove it was not as potent as English bitter! It seemed, he said later, like a good idea at the time!

The beer had a 5 per cent alcohol content and eventually made its mark. How that content compared with English bitter I have no idea but I would guess it to be slightly stronger. Dismal could hardly stand but still insisted he was capable of drinking "sodee-pop" until daylight. Alas, when daylight came, he had long since been tucked into bed and was well past the caring stage! Someone, he swore, had spiked his drinks!

Dismal did not have many virtues but he had one that was outstanding. He *never* broke a promise. He was always punctual and totally reliable. Like me, he had no time for those who turned up late.

"Time is time," he would say. And he would set off alone rather than wait for latecomers. We had that much in common, if little else.

Despite our different lifestyles, however, Dismal remained a close friend and loyal companion for over 60 years. I still have memories of him standing up to his knees in Walton Pond in Aylesbury and demanding to know what time it was and how he got there.

He had apparently reached his predicament after a lengthy session, with a $4^{1}/_{2}$ gallon keg of old ale. When he had seen it arrive he had claimed it for his own, paid for it and, as he put it, "supped the lot". Thirty-six pints of old ale, quaffed in one all-night and half-day-long session, might kill the average tippler. Dismal complained merely that he was tired. I am tempted to add – "as a newt"!

In later years, he lived with his aged mother and looked after her to the best of his ability. He was, by then, partly disabled but still retained his love of good food and drink.

Always his favourite meal was prime rib of beef on the bone with Yorkshire pudding, roast potatoes and fresh vegetables from his small garden. So it was that on a certain lunchtime several years ago he carved the Sunday joint, passed his mother's plate and sat down to enjoy his own. His head dropped forward and, without a sound, Dismal left this world.

I doubt if he ever regretted any part of his life and in all the years I knew him I never heard him complain with true bitterness.

His sense of humour was such that I know he would never take offence at the remark made by a mutual friend after his death.

"The Good Lord took him in good style," he said. "But He might have let him finish his dinner first!"

Jerk it!"

I did not know his name and, in any event, it happened a long time ago. He was an aged Minnesotan and he was having trouble teaching a youngster how to fish for bluegills. The boy was too slow to strike and consequently missed fish after fish.

"You gotta jerk it, boy!" he said.

"But I am jerking it, Grandpa," junior insisted.

The aged one struck with his own tackle and landed yet another bluegill.

"See what I mean, boy," he beamed. "You gotta jerk it – just before they bite!"

6
KEN

Ken was once referred to by the legendary Dick Walker as the "most joyous member of a joyous crew". He was a superb fly tier, a tench fishing expert, a perch specialist, a boat handler of extraordinary skill, and he had a sense of humour as dry as prairie dust. He was a practical man but he was also a dreamer who loved to lie between two carp rods under the everlasting stars. He could be shy at times but just occasionally he would wax eloquent on piscatorial topics. He helped many youngsters catch their first fish. He loved campfires, wild places and his fellow men. He was known to almost every freshwater angler of his generation in the country and I never, in a lifetime, heard anyone say a bad word about him. He fished with me in several different parts of the world and I could not have asked for a better fishing buddy. He was one of "The Taylor Brothers". He was my "kid" brother and he died on September 15th 1991.

That he has a place in the scheme of things regarding this book is unlikely to be disputed, least of all by me, but today I wonder just what aspects of his fishing life are best portrayed.

He *was* an expert angler. In particular he was an expert trout angler as well as someone who could hold his own alongside other experts in almost any freshwater situation. On reflection it has to be said that he was not highly competitive. He would occasionally compete at a local level but he was not a match angler by any means. His expertise had to do with his ability to handle tackle and how to "read" a situation. He would have been at a disadvantage within the confines of a ten-yard peg. He had to roam free and find his fish. "Today is a perch day," he would say with conviction. And he would be right. "There is a roach swim," he would say, pointing at a streamy run he had never seen before. And he would prove it before the day ended.

He read avidly of those literary items which increased his own knowledge but he had a way of absorbing fresh information quietly and of finding a situation to use it long after it had first appeared.

I will, of course, remember him for his sheer enthusiasm and how he (some six years younger and freshly demobbed from the Royal Navy where he had served on the horrendous Russian convoys) never stopped bending my ear about his fishing plans after World War II.

It is hard now to believe that our rods in those days were converted tank aerials, that our reels were wooden centre-pins, or that our only forms of transport were our pushbikes. No-one, however, could have enjoyed fishing more.

If anyone asked me to recall "red-letter" days with Ken, I could do so without a moment's hesitation. My only problem would have to do with which red-letter days to include and which ones to omit. There were so many. And, in truth, few if any had to do with the big fish or big catches he took more or less for granted. Most of them had to do with the magic of the moment and the company of the special friends involved.

Ken lived quite close to the Aylesbury arm of the Grand Union Canal and tended to fish there alone during the summer evenings simply for reasons of convenience. I flogged away at the lake and pits on the opposite side of town for the same reason. Eventually, however, we teamed up to fish for the tench of Claydon Lakes which involved 17 miles of pedal pushing each way. We learned there that there was more to tench fishing than "laying on" with worms or big paste baits. Those tactics worked for a time but we proved, to our own satisfaction, there and later at Halton and Wotton, that a busy style, using smaller baits (including what are today referred to as particles) would invariably produce more tench.

At Wotton Lakes the catches of tench recorded by the so-called Taylor Brothers were very much above the national average and Ken's regular contributions to the general scheme of things were considerable.

His carpentry skills and his knowledge of boats in general helped us to transform an old and derelict army bridge pontoon into a super fishing boat on which we lived for days at a time. I recall the heavy loads of timber, paint, tools and other merchandise we loaded on to three converted errand bikes to keep us occupied for all twelve weekends of the close season. We lived but 14 miles distant but we worked from dawn until dark and slept wherever we found shelter. Always we asked Ken what the next task would be. Always he would take care of those needing the greater skills.

We were exhausted at times but our evening meal was always eaten around our "campfire". Ken was a romantic. He saw pictures in the flames and he saw weird creatures in the shadows of the trees around us.

I shared so many magic moments with Ken but the very best of them were almost invariably shared around a campfire. Ken would conjure up memories from the flickering flames and we would talk on when we should have been sleeping.

I know that one of the highlights of his life came when he joined the late Ted Trueblood and me where the Oregon desert and the mountains of Owyhee are separated only by a narrow strip of water some 50 miles long and averaging a mile across. It holds countless bays and inlets and we chose one of those remote spots for our base camp. In the eight days we were there we saw only three other humans. Three dots on the horizon could be discerned through binoculars as three mounted cowboys.

Ken revelled in the heat and dust of that desolate country. He fished his heart out during the day for bass and crappie. He tumbled off the boat into the water when the heat (it was recorded as 127°F in the shade and there we had no shade whatsoever!) became too much to take. At night he would prepare the campfire from driftwood and, while we all helped with the camp chores, he would set up a couple of bait rods and let them fish for themselves. Baits were fish portions; the quarry was channel catfish or brown bullheads.

"This is how Huckleberry Finn used to do it," he said as he sat on a rock with his feet in the water, waiting for his tiny spinning rod to bend downwards. When it did he would crank in yet another small catfish and remark that "breakfast was looking good".

While Ted snored in his old camp truck and I lay in my sleeping bag, Ken would kick the fire back into life and gaze into the flames. Who knows what his thoughts were? Those were days and nights of sheer joy during his lifetime which later held little else but tragedy. I will always be glad that I was able to tempt him from his busy life to spend three weeks in the great American outdoors. I was never in any doubt that he was equally glad. It was always his favourite talking point.

When we built the Fishing Hut on the upper Great Ouse, it was Ken who actually built it. He prefabricated it. We put it together on site with his help and under his guidance. The Fishing Hut was Ken's pride and joy. Many others helped to dig foundations, pour concrete, lay tiles and wield paint brushes. The late Dick Walker, who financed the whole project, declared himself foreman since he appeared for the most part to sit and give orders but, in fact, Ken was accepted as General Foreman from start to finish. The Fishing Hut was his "baby".

We stayed overnight on many occasions during the building of the hut and once again campfires featured in our working pleasures. The river was crawling with crayfish and we would cook them by the gallon and eat them as we talked into the darkness.

Ken went with Dick to fill the water pot one day. The river then was clean and unpolluted. It had not been vandalised by dredging and abstraction. We swam in it and drank from it with no fears of the consequences. Somehow or other Ken lost his footing and went fully clothed into the river. It was not a total submersion but the next best thing to it. He threw out a hand, Dick grabbed it and hauled a dripping Ken back on to the bank.

"Cor, thanks Dick," said Ken. "I'd have been wet through if you hadn't saved me." Such was his sense of humour.

I think perhaps that I was responsible for Ken becoming a night fisher simply because I could never patiently wait for the dawn. Ken did not need a great deal of persuading, however, and although I have enjoyed many nights with many fishing companions, I know I was never more content than when he and I had the night and the water to ourselves.

With our floats lit up in torch beams we fished for bream, tench and eels at "The Hawthornes" in Lincolnshire. In total darkness with bait and fly rods, we fished the magical little Cumbrian Esk, courtesy of Hugh Falkus who left us to do our own thing.

"Why should people want to sleep on a night like this?" Ken would ask quietly above the chuckling of dub's shallow water. And once, as we made our way back to camp at dawn and saw the first rays of the sun appear over the top of the crag, he remarked, "Whether you believe in God or not, it's hard to imagine that all this is DIY." I never really forgot that, but then there is so much of the man that I will always remember.

His love of seclusion and the escape from civilisation caused us to prolong our fishing season and to stay overnight at certain waters where we could unroll a sleeping bag in reasonable comfort. One such place was an old boathouse in Lincolnshire where we were allowed to install a paraffin heater and a simple bottle-gas cooker for our convenience. Ken's reluctance to discontinue night fishing led us to fishing for pike after dark. Along with many, or most, other anglers, we believed that pikes' predations ceased when darkness fell, but we learned differently after he suggested that we should "find out for ourselves".

Off the verandah of that old staging we cast deadbaits into the night. The kettle boiled on the heater, the third member

47

of our party (one Al Pond) decided that "Saturday night without a few beers was not on" and drove off to the village. He returned later with a case of canned beer and a bottle of Scotch!

The rest of the night should, perhaps, be forgotten. Ken was not strictly a drinking man at the time but he entered into the spirit of things by drinking the first beer and looping his line around the empty can. When it hit the decking, he assured us, he would know he had hooked a pike. All we need do was sit back in the warm and await events. Soon, all three pike lines were looped around beer cans. The first-ever night bite-alarm for pike had been invented!

We caught quite a few pike that night. If I remember correctly they were all over 10lb and several were (in today's angling parlance) high doubles. Every so often a beer can hit the wooden flooring and all three of us would rush to see whose bait had been taken. There was great excitement around the heater for a time but it did not last.

It's yours," said Al, when a beer can clanked in the early morning hours.

"It's Fred's," said Ken, pouring a generous measure of Scotch.

I decided it was time to quit and wound in all three tackles.

"It seemed like a good idea at the time," said Al next morning, holding his head.

"For pity's sake put the kettle on, someone," I begged.

"I thought we were having pike for breakfast," said Ken. "I'll be back." He grabbed a rod, pushed out the leaky punt and rowed out into the nigh-frozen lake.

He came back half an hour later with a four-pounder which he tossed in my direction.

"You cook it; I'll peel the spuds," was all he said.

I never knew if it was sheer bravado on his part or whether he was simply not suffering the hangover he deserved! I loved him but I never quite understood him.

Ken lost his only son in January 1991 and I watched him switch off the world and slowly die of a broken heart.

"We three," he often told me, indicating his wife Pat and his son Richard (named after Dick Walker), "are a small community all on our own."

Three days after his funeral, news came to me that his wife had died in hospital.

I shed no tears when Ken died. I knew he would not want me to weep. He would want me to remember the hilarious times we had together and the love of the outdoors we so often shared. No-one will ever know how many silent tears I have shed since, however. Tears of sorrow because I miss him so much. Tears of anger because I cannot believe he deserved such torment and suffering. Tears of frustration because I was totally unable to prevent it!

While Ken and his family were with us they were indeed a small community on their own. Today, with God's good grace, perhaps, they are reunited as a much happier one. A certain faith convinces me that is so.

7
MURGETT

To me he will always be Frank because that is his name. Frank Murgett. To most of the rest of the angling world (at least to those old enough to remember his early exploits) he will always be known as Murgett. Where to start and end this chapter about one of the most remarkable characters I have ever met, causes me immediate problems. There is so much to write; so little space in which to write it.

Perhaps I should make it clear at the outset that I admire the man's writings. Or at least I admire them when he has his writing hat firmly in place. When he allows it to slip (as we all do on occasions) his work can be abrasive. It can also knock the occasional rooster off his crowing perch and for that we should all give thanks!

Frank Murgett, I feel, is a man of moods and that very fact puts him high up on my list of angling writers. His moods, whether he realises it or not, bring out the best of him. He will always command my respect but I know that he would never expect me always to agree with his sentiments. Perhaps that is why we have remained friends for so many years.

I met him first in the early 1950s when we were both writing regularly for that lovely old magazine, alas now defunct, *The Anglers' News*.

The so-called Taylor Brothers (i.e. my brother Ken, my cousin Joe and myself) were catching big bags of tench from Wotton Lakes in the early 1950s and, as we were more or less colleagues in print, I invited Frank to join us.

He went out of his way then to portray a totally laid-back image and to convince us that he was an arrogant know-all. I hated him at first sight, and when he cranked in a $3^1/_2$lb tench on heavy gear and tossed it back in "over his shoulder", I hated him even more. So did Ken and Joe, but we were too polite to tell him what we thought of him.

"How are they for tackle here?" he had asked. "I'm just back from tope fishing. Haven't had time to put on a new line. This one's 16lb breaking strain."

And we, who revered our tench as much as today's carp angler reveres his carp, saw a yob, a lout, an insensitive oaf on our lovely boat reviling our lovely tench. We ought to have known better! Perhaps it was just as well that we did not react as we might have done in the circumstances. Had we done so, a friendship would not have developed. It became apparent, after we had silently fumed for a short time, that this dreadful "townie" was in fact winding us up for all he was worth.

He took our hero Richard Walker to pieces strip by strip and he made a mockery of carp and those who fished for them. He claimed that he never fished at night and that those who did, simply slept by their rods until their bite alarms sounded.

In those early days of electric bite alarm development there were many home-made affairs but nothing in the way of a commercial product. We all tried to improve on the original invented by Richard Walker but we failed. Frank Murgett insisted that Walker was presently engaged in producing a new one which allowed him to sleep all night but blew "reveille" in the morning! Only one of the earlier carp fishers would recognise the deadliness of such an insult! In those days we regarded it as sinfully unsporting to fall asleep by our rods and we tried desperately to keep awake all night.

Despite his avowed hatred of night fishing, however, Frank Murgett told us about his penny-in-a-jam-jar bite alarm.

Make no mistake about it. The idea was simple and brilliant. The line was laid under a penny balanced on a jam-jar lip. A pull on the bait flipped the penny into the jar and the tinkle awoke the angler from his reverie. His contrived behaviour on our pontoon boat gave us the impression that he not only hated night fishing but that he had no love for carp either. He almost fooled us into believing him but, later, Joe and I accepted an invitation to fish for the wild carp at Wadhurst as his guest.

We had to travel by train as far as London and be picked up somewhere near Liverpool Street on the Friday evening. Bearing in mind that we had to end our weekly labours before setting forth, it was not easy to be there by the appointed hour of 6.30 p.m.

We made it with our rucksacks, tent, waders, tackle and bait. We had to forego the luxuries of sleeping bags, air beds and other truly essential items in the interest of weight. The way we planned it was to sit up and fish both nights and sleep during the daytime. It is a good plan when "travelling light" is of top priority, and it works very well indeed if the weather remains fine and warm. It is horrendous when cold and relentless rain greets one at the waterside.

Plans to fish by the rods all night went by the board. Joe and I pitched tent and tried to keep dry during the night, but it was a lost cause. A dose of sheer misery is the only way that night could be described, and Murgett, having decided to "kip down because there would be nothing doing tonight", retired to his van to spend the night in comfort snuggled up to his lovely old German Shepherd dog!

I caught a carp at dawn next morning when Murgett did a strange war dance on the bank in order to "put his beams across".

"You'll get a carp any minute now," he informed me. And I did. The line began to strip off the spool and I landed a 4-pounder.

"Told yer," he said. "It's me beams!"

He did not know it then (and I am only confessing now because I might just be beginning to understand the man!) that it was my best ever carp to date. Laugh if you like, but a carp was a carp in those days and I was a happy man.

I was also a very wet man. So was Joe and so was all the gear we had brought with us.

Is there anything more soul-destroying than striking a wet camp? If there is I do not want to know about it! As we tried to pack our gear, however, and while Frank scraped off his whiskers, his line began to strip off the spool. I do not recall ever actually "hearing" line strip off a spool before but this run produced a hiss that could be heard from where we stood. Frank continued to shave. We shouted, stamped our feet, waved our arms and hopped around in panic. Frank carried on shaving! Eventually he ambled down to the water's edge and cranked in a carp about as big as the one I had caught the previous day.

"What's so bloody clever about that then?" he asked. "There's nothing to this carp fishing. Walker makes it *seem* difficult but there's nothing to it really. Some carp take bread; some don't. Those that do get caught."

Was it a wind-up? Was he secretly pleased to have caught a carp, however insignificant, during the last hour or so at the water?

I doubt if we'll ever know. Frank Murgett could put on an innocent expression guaranteed to keep anyone guessing. I suspect that it pleased him to see me catch a carp. I suspect it also pleased him to catch one just as big. But I am prepared to believe that he could easily shrug both incidents off as unimportant by saying that anyone could catch a carp if he wanted to. Corse he could!

He has since referred to that lake as a "little jewel of a place in a green, sweet valley" and I think back to those days with affection.

Then we were beginning to accept that it made sense to dip into our fishing waters instead of hauling tap water around in heavy bottles. Wotton's water was fine; so was that of the upper Great Ouse.

Redmire's was undrinkable since it tasted like fish paste! Other waters were acceptable but we who tried the water of the "little jewel" found indeed that it made the finest of brews. It was the acid in it, Frank told us, and it's a fair bet he was right.

When I cross the bridge over the Ouse today I shudder to think what would happen to those who dipped in it and drank from it as we did. It is all so very sad and we who have access to other "little jewels" are lucky in that they are unlikely to be affected by sewage or silage effluents. We should give thanks but we should also be on our guard. Waters are lost to causes other than pollution!

Petty officialdom can do strange things and "safe" waters can suddenly become very much endangered. The system can seldom be beaten except, perhaps, when waters are purchased outright by those interested in fishing them.

The Carp Society has already become involved in purchasing its own waters and, as a result, future fishing is further protected. It will now be more difficult for those waters to be designated as rubbish tips by those who wield the ungodly powers of local government. But, of course, they will try. Just as they did when Frank Murgett ran a successful and reputable maggot factory in Bucks a few years after we first met. They were determined to close him down and they succeeded because those they indoctrinated believed sincerely that maggots caused health hazards. Maggots were spoilers of food and therefore enemies of society. That belief, said Frank at the time, was engraved in man's memory for all time. The officials knew better but they were relentless and ruthless. Frank had to go.

I tried to help fight his case in the local paper but it was hopeless. Rumours were spread to foil my efforts. An allotment holder swore that if he dug deeply enough blood seeped up from the maggot factory three fields away on the other side of the river!

Frank added fuel to their protests by ridiculing those who sought to destroy him. It was untrue, he said, that cows dropped dead two miles from the building. Or that pilots lost in fog as they approached London Airport homed in on the smell of the maggotarium! He would not, you see, offer any sign of servility. He was his own man and if our regular correspondence is any indication, he still is today.

His letters are a delight because he cares not for the finer points of grammar and deliberately flouts them to make a point. His writings are what I would term as "brave" simply because he will not bow to tradition. He will split an infinitive and quote Omar Khayyam or Shakespeare in the same sentence, but the reader knows at all times that the errors he makes are deliberate. That ability rates very highly in my estimation.

I could write a whole book on Frank Murgett but this chapter on the man has to end somewhere. Perhaps a short extract from a recent letter from him may provide me with the beginning of the end.

"So, to conclude my missive, feel free to use and do what you will if you think that such a carelessly humble disciple of the art as I merits attention, for at no time have I ever used fishing other than in the way it should be used ... viz. as a carelessly enjoyable thing which took me to pleasant places, doing pleasant things in the best of company selected and grown together in compatibility and love of the fishing game. I can bravely say that I have never taken fishing all that seriously and at times I have been downright sloppy and careless and lazy. I can even recall days when I have not even taken my rods out of the bag after travelling umpteen miles. I can recall other days when I have behaved quite idiotically and wandered into wild and snowy places on my own where, truth to tell, I might still be had I been stricken by some unfortunate happening, and fished all night and motored and opened up a business in the morning and done a day's work like the best of angling idiots.

"What an erratic creature I was, here and there set and determined to win the club match and all the cups if I could, or catch a big fish if I could, and then go quite the other way. In other words, use the fishing game, and lean on a stile or a bridge parapet and watch the chub cruise idly round, or lay as I did once I well recall, out in the wilds. Just lay, my rod in the water and the sun shining down over sheep and green fields, just lay until my brother came and asked, 'What are you thinking about?'

"And I said dreamily, 'Well, I'm just enjoying the moment.

I am in no pain, I have money, and no worries to speak of other than those which are every man's lot. I have a family and a sweet daughter at home, and I wish my dog was here with me, but she isn't and the weather is warm and I've caught three nice tench and now, well, I'm just enjoying what I've got.' "

That, perhaps, sums up the man better than any words of mine.

I have not seen Frank Murgett for many years and I am quite sure we shall never fish together again. I am not concerned about that fact since we are two different creatures and time has possibly mellowed us both.

I swear, however, that I am going to make the effort, if the Good Lord allows it, to go down to Kent and sink a glass of ale with him before we're both too old to appreciate it!

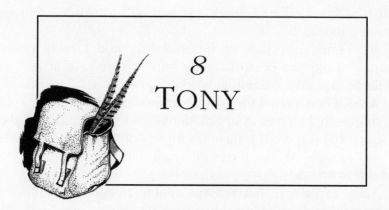

8
TONY

My friendship with Tony Francis began in an odd way and, truth to tell, it is a minor miracle that it ever got past first base!

A telephoned message from Kingfisher Television asked if I could help with a programme featuring ferrets. (I was, and still am, interested in, and seen as someone knowledgeable about, these charming animals.)

Having had only frustrating experiences with TV productions in the past, I was hesitant but, since I was currently involved with the formation and promotion of a National Society concerned with ferrets and their image, I saw an opportunity.

I suggested that the cameras and the producer should join me and about 200 ferrets at a Country Show near Milton Keynes, Bucks. I had but one simple, sincere condition. Please do *NOT* portray the ferret as a vicious creature, likely to bite anything and everything in sight. Our newly formed Society's dream was to convince the rest of the world that ferrets were NOT smelly, evil, untrustworthy creatures, but that, like all other domestic animals, they responded to kindness!

I proved it at the time by convincing the late Johnny Morris ("The Animal Man", who was scared witless!) that if a little girl of seven years old could pick up a brace of jill (female) ferrets and bring them to him, there was no need for fear. Johnny was hesitant but, to his credit, he ended up having ferrets in his shirt and up the arms of his jacket. He was amazed but totally persuaded regarding the nature of these quiet mustelids!

We filmed all kinds of ferret activity and I went home happy at the prospect of seeing ferrets portrayed, at last, as reliable and understanding, working pets.

Alas! When Tony introduced the final programme, he held a strange hob ferret in a gauntlet-gloved hand and told the viewer that this would "have his fingers off" given the chance! I was furious! All our ferret PR work was wasted as a result of a few seconds' erroneous publicity!

Tony explained that he was simply trying to be "devil's advocate" and, once our differences had been sorted out, we became good friends and have remained so since.

Today I appear frequently on his *Heart of the Country* and *Carlton Country* programmes, and the title of this book has been blatantly stolen from it – simply because I cannot think of a better one! I find it hard to believe that we have worked together for ten years!

That his programme has been running for over ten years is proof enough that he knows his job *and* knows exactly what he wants!

His skills amount to a genius and most people know that those with such ingenuity are not always easy to please! I think I can say that we are good friends and that his wife and mine hit it off (which is a bonus *not* always applicable!) but it is a fact that our friendship has had to weather a few storms!

The trouble with TV producers, and some of those associated with them, is that, being perfectionists, they seek perfection from all those they employ. This is where problems begin to appear. I am wise enough *not* to commit myself at any stage unless I am positive I can make good my boast. There is no other way around the situation! Homework is the answer. Homework well in advance.

Tony once paid me the compliment of telling a member of the crew that "if Fred says it will be OK, I know that it will be"! That, perhaps, is my forté and part of my own serious attempt at perfection. If Tony says – for instance – that tomorrow he expects me to harvest (by any means) a couple of rabbits and cook them in my Dutch oven over a campfire, I will quietly decline. Murphy's Law would make sure I failed and that, in terms of TV, would be an expensive failure! Unlike some other colleagues who promise the earth just to be "on the box", I prefer to take out some kind of insurance! I'll have a couple of rabbits on ice on the day of filming! *Then*, because it does not matter, wild rabbits will line up to be caught! That's how *I* have succeeded for ten years or more! How can anyone, with any country experience, promise to show – say – a kingfisher, a carp, a heron, a kestrel or whatever at a certain time on a certain day? It doesn't happen that way! It all takes a great deal of time, and time costs money, so I have made a practice of being truthful! And it has paid dividends.

None of such suggests that making any programme is easy, that incredible luck or sheer dedication, on the part of the employee, is ever likely to be understood or appreciated by producers. They have a hard time of it. Their underlings may find life even tougher!

The difference is, I feel, that the employees, while prepared to strive for perfection, expect the occasional failure. The professional producer looks for, and expects, precision at all times. And he (or she) does not recognise sheer luck and the gifts from the gods as and when they bounce his way. I can claim some very serious examples of sheer luck on TV. My old friend Bill Hughes insisted that I was born under a lucky star and, whether such a thing is possible or not, I have to accept that I have had my fair share of good fortune.

Producers, because they are not anglers, for instance, have always failed to recognise or appreciate the great fortunes bestowed upon them by Lady Luck herself.

I do not have to go into detail to make the average carp man understand that having video cameras concentrated on an angler in the middle of the afternoon, at the precise moment when a 15-pounder decides to take the bait, involves more than a mere smidgen of luck!

My young friend, Alan Young, came up with the goods on an otherwise desperate and desolate day. It was sheer magic. It would have been so to any carp angler worth his salt, but it received a mere shrug of the shoulders from the lovely lady TV producer who replaced Tony on the day. She had expected more action than that, despite the fact that I warned her time and again that we would be lucky even to see a carp on that bleak and uncompromising day!

Compare that lack of enthusiasm with another incredible slice of luck and you will see what I mean.

Cold, wet, miserable and uncomfortable, I sat in a boat on the Red River in Manitoba. In another boat, a few yards away, a camera crew told us to sock it to the carp that were reputedly present. We were on a licking to nothing and we knew it. The river was like brown Windsor soup and the centre channel was a raging torrent.

The Red River flows north and this venture was taking place a few days after horrendous floods had hit the middle west of the United States. The great lock gates were all open and were being swept downstream like so much kindling. It was, if I'm honest, a frightening and totally frustrating situation. An occasional back fin broke the surface of our sheltered area but, as the mud swirled in angry clouds from the bottom, I got the impression that those fish were showing in discomfort rather than in wild abandon!

It is often suggested that fish seen "topping" in the swim gives an indication of a feeding pattern about to commence. In the Red River it is particularly true when conditions are half-normal but, on the day in question, fishing to order was a nightmare. No sooner had the cameras lined up than one or other of the anchors would slip and cause the boat to face the opposite (more or less) direction. We did our best and sheer persistence paid off in the end. There came an occasional clearing or fining down of the current, which left the baited swim with much less mud in suspension for a matter of minutes. I cannot figure out exactly how it happened, except to say that as the current built up it piled more mud into the area. As it slackened off (as often happens in flood conditions) it allowed the mud to settle.

During a few of those periods of relief, we hooked into several carp up to about 15lb. Not big but, in the circumstances, more than welcome. At least we had not failed to catch at all! When it became obvious that we were not going to improve on the score, we went back to shore and established a bank swim which would allow the cameras better control while still giving them opportunity to film Stu McKay, who was fishing for catfish in a boat 100 yards or so from where we sat.

What followed has to be regarded as a classic example of luck deserved only by the chosen few! This does not in any way detract from Stu McKay's great skills as a catfish angler. It merely makes clear that to be present and on the button with cameras set, when *any* fish is caught, can only be regarded as a bonus. To be up and running when a near-record fish hangs on may suggest devilish collusion to some who have been the route! I have been there and I know the problems! Stu was into a fish and his light, soft-actioned rod was bent almost double.

"Give it some welly," I yelled from the bank.

"I can't, Fred," came the reply. "This rod's not man enough."

I knew that Stu is somewhat blasé about catfish. He has caught so many. This one, however, was giving him trouble and our mutual friend Pete McKenzie offered to take the camera crew out in his boat to film the whole sequence. It is to his credit that he kept the cameras on the subject by sheer and total boat control. He kept the platform steady, he outwitted every move made by the fish and, when the anchor rope was pulled to prevent loss of an obvious specimen, he followed at close quarters without taking chances. We, who watched, realised the important part he played and, accordingly, gave him credit. It is extremely doubtful, however, if the programme makers will even remember his existence! He has my personal thanks anyway.

The catfish took about 45 minutes to boat. I saw it break surface a couple of times and, even at that distance, it was awesome. "It could well be a 40-pounder," I estimated to those around me and, as it turned out, I was not far wrong. It weighed $39\frac{1}{2}$lb, and was the second largest catfish ever taken from Canadian waters!

Our reactions, having been involved from start to finish, were "Wow! How about that then? What will Tony have to say about *that* when he flies in tomorrow?"

We had worked well on our own. Each knew his task and Jayne, the lovely continuity lady who had guided us through the tricky bits, was rightly happy!

We were bubbling when we reported the day's proceedings, but we should have known not to wax enthusiastic. We were met with a kind of blank disappointment regarding our catfish success.

"What? Only the one?" said Tony.

I guess there really is no answer to that but it *does* tend to cut you down to size! If you let it, that is.

From my own point of view I have to say that I was paid to do a job and that I did it to the best of my ability, and to the absolute delight of several of the Canadian Tourist Board officials who shared some of our simple pleasures.

Tony filmed beavers at work and play, eagles and otters, bears and buffalo, turtles and muskrats, loons, ravens, pelicans, wild geese and fish of many species, including carp and pike which, though not new to us in Britain, are different in so many respects.

We shared a campfire with a dozen or more guests from here and there. We ate roast duck and roast pork and damper from the Dutch oven; we drank freely of Canadian wine, beer and rye whisky; and we revelled in the resplendence of the Canadian bush, 100 miles from nowhere across the Winnipeg River. It was an experience I can hardly wait to repeat and I plan to do so again and again for as long as the Good Lord allows it.

I truly thought we were incredibly lucky to achieve what we did in the few days of grace at our disposal. So many, many, ordinary folk live a whole lifetime without seeing a hint of what we saw in that brief period and I know I can say, without any embarrassment, that I gave thanks for the privilege. There really *is* more to fishing than the size and numbers game but it is essential to be able to recognise luck when it comes!

Tony said later, on the phone, that he thought it had been a bit disappointing! All of which tends to prove that you can't please *all* of the people *all* of the time! *And* that TV producers, in the main, *are* not prepared to admit to luck. That is a pity since our particular crew have had more than their fair share and that, despite all, Tony and I have remained good friends.

"Slow Poison"

His name was Walter Carter. He lived in Lancashire
and his friends called him the water cart – though it is
doubtful if water formed a very big part of his diet. He
liked bitter ale and drank three pints in the same pub
every night.

"You ought to slow down on that stuff," one of his
younger acquaintances once insisted. "That's slow
poison if you did but know it."

"I know it is," said Walter. "Slow indeed! I'm 84. I've
been drinking it since I was 14 and I'm still here. That's
bloody slow, if you ask me."

9
QUINCY

Quincy, they said, had short arms and deep pockets. He was either slow at paying his round or he "had no money on him" at the time.

He was an excellent rabbiter and he loved fishing for eels, largely, one suspects, because he loved a "bowl of jellied". He was not a strict harvester of wild food but he was a hunter and an opportunist. He was, without doubt, a poacher and an extremely good shot with a game gun. He never owned a gun in his life to my knowledge but, somehow or other, he managed to borrow whatever he needed and the necessary cartridges to go with it.

He was a good man with ferrets and took great pride in "working the line" because that is where he truly excelled. Not every ferreting person will be aware of the great skill involved in using a lined or tethered ferret correctly. The process is too complicated to describe fully but the simple theory is that a lined, male ferret will track down a female ferret with her kill underground and take over from her until relieved by diggers from above.

In practice it is not quite that simple and there are operators who, somehow or other, acquire a special sense about the whole procedure and turn it into an art form. Quincy was one such person. He was always in demand to "work the line" when big rabbit clearance jobs were envisaged. He did his job well and no-one begrudged him the odd pint in the local afterwards. Over a long period, however, this "got no money on me" excuse became very noticeable.

Quincy was lying head downwards over a deep ditch one day working the line, as was his practice. Brumby, on his hands and knees in the dry ditch bottom, found a pile of silver and copper that had obviously fallen out of Quincy's pocket. There was about fifteen shillings worth of change all told (a lot of pocket money in those early post-war days!) and Brumby pocketed the lot!

When pub-time arrived, Quincy apologised again for having no money on him. He was, he said, stony broke and had been all week. Brumby told him not to worry. He had picked up fifteen bob at the bottom of the ditch, he said, and that should keep the three of us in ale until closing time! At about a shilling a pint (5 pence by today's standards) it was more than enough! Quincy was strangely quiet for the rest of the day!

He had a big family and it is to his credit that he did his best to provide for it. The problem was that he did not like going home empty-handed. Like the lovely big, old, black Labrador retriever, beloved of my good friend Peter Thomas, he had to return with something. Ross, the Labrador, would bring back anything, from the shot quarry to a desperate moorhen, or an empty cartridge case. Quincy would bring anything from a lamb to half a sackful of potatoes and vegetables.

On his night-time, long-netting ventures, he encountered many creatures, and his razor-sharp knife took care of many an unwary lamb. In today's world of full and plenty, that is, perhaps, inexcusable behaviour, but I always found it hard to disagree with Quincy's assertion that the lamb was never even missed!

Nor, if the truth be told, were the bags of potatoes, turnips, kale, field beans and other vegetables that were picked from time to time on Quincy's hunting forays. I cannot stand on a soap box to defend his action, but I can claim to understand them. I wonder, if *I* would stand by and see *my* family go hungry in the same circumstances? Only those who have known hard times themselves should be allowed to condemn others for being opportunists.

Quincy rode a lady's bicycle which, let it be said, had been abandoned in many ditches on many occasions while he made his escape from pheasant coverts on foot! The fact that it was a lady's bike always intrigued us and in the end we were obliged to demand an explanation.

The story he told us was as follows. Late one night, he had been returning from a long-netting venture when he had encountered a charming young lady cyclist in trouble. Her chain had broken and she was somewhat distressed. He had repaired the broken chain and made sure that the lovely lady had not been obliged to dirty her hands or clothes. She lived only a mile or so away and he had accompanied her to her cottage, where he had been allowed to wash his hands and tidy himself up generally.

The lady, he said, was grateful. She showered and joined him, clad in a dressing gown to express her appreciation. She was so relieved, she said, that Quincy could ask for anything he wanted as a reward. Anything at all, she insisted.

Quincy thought it over, decided it was too good an opportunity to miss, and chose to accept her bike! He pointed to it.

"There it is," he said. "Still going strong after all these years."

You could catch Quincy out for some of the time but for most of it he was a born winner!

10
LES

Just as a matter of interest, and mentioned purely in passing, Les Webber is a fine angler. He would not strut around telling you so because he has more important things in life to consider than his personal best fish, including carp of 38lb, perch of 4lb 10oz, and pike up to 28lb. He sees a great deal more in fishing than fish safely on the bank and, unlike many others with fewer qualifications, he is not an ego-tripper. Far from it. He keeps himself to himself for most of the time but he is deeply concerned with the promotion of fishing – particularly with youngsters in mind. He has an interesting story to tell but will not tell it unless pressed into doing so – as I have found out in the few years I have known him.

Like many others of his era, he started fishing as a kid of eleven years with a cane rod and a cotton reel. That fact alone was a revelation to me, since I can still remember fashioning a greenhouse tomato cane, and a cotton reel loaded with thread, in order to fish the River Severn at Worcester. I was convalescing there at the age of 25 after being evacuated from France a couple of months after D Day!

In today's world of carbons and rod pods, such equipment would be laughable and yet, as Les told me at our last meeting, there is always great joy to be derived from improvisation. I know. I have been the route myself many times! In 1977 Les took over as Leisure Sport Angling Club's special projects co-ordinator. He started the group (as it is known today) Angling Projects TP with the help of Jack Ashby in 1983.

Les told me of the disused building that was designated to them by the late Terry Catliff, who was a director of Leisure Sport Angling in 1986. A great opportunity for the development of a pipe dream Les had held for many years. Here was a wooden building that would make a club house for the promotion of angling, friendship and conservation among those with fewer opportunities than most.

The conditions were simple.

1) The building had to be maintained.

2) It had to be self-financing along with the group itself.

3) It had to be used for youngsters from all walks of life.

Leisure Sport Angling agreed not to use the building as a venue for their own business and presented it totally free of charge to Angling Projects. Sadly, and almost undoubtedly as a result of vandalism, the building was totally destroyed by fire in July 1990. There was no insurance involved and some £20,000 of gear was destroyed.

The soul of many a lesser mortal might well also have been destroyed but not so the soul of Les Webber. He was devastated but not defeated and he set to work with the rebuilding of the property in 1991.

It has been my privilege to see the development in its several stages and I have been astonished always at the total dedication of Les and his happy band of volunteers. Those men – for men they surely are – have shovelled sand and gravel, hauled breeze blocks and timber, laid foundations, poured concrete, paved the walkways, laid tiles, fitted toilets, refrigerators, stoves, microwave units and furniture, and are presently engaged in painting and decorating both inside and outside of that very substantial unit.

Throughout it all labour costs have been zero. Material costs, thanks to the goodwill created by Les and his happy band, have been more or less the same. Les refers to his helpers as "The Team". They work when they might well be fishing, and they give their time without thoughts of payment. They are, as Dick Walker might have put it, a joyous crew.

In any venture of this kind a great deal of scrounging has to be on the agenda and obviously the building, when it is finally completed (probably by the time this appears in print), will be a monument to those who donated paint, tiles, cement, machinery and a host of other materials towards its fulfilment.

I have been there, on the banks of that small but prolific lake at Wraysbury, on a number of occasions to see Les Webber pushing a mower over the closely cropped grass around the bank. *I* know the going is tough. *I* know that all this work goes on a long way from Les's home in Reading, and I know that Les's wife has to be a very tolerant lady. He and I are, I believe, similarly blessed in that respect. Which, perhaps, is just as well.

I suggested that shoving a mower over a defined area of bank space was asking a lot from a man who ran his own business and worked hard all week. Les agreed that it was getting tougher as the years passed by but confirmed that he intended to maintain the site and the fishing to the best of his ability. Someone at that stage suggested that we should hold a sheep roast to raise funds for the purchase of a "sit-on" mower. I thought the idea was sound and felt confident that I could organise such an event in due course.

Les agreed in principle. Lovely idea, he said. But there were other things needed by the projects group and he would, for the time being at least, continue to push away at his task. The money, he said, could be put to better use. Who am I to argue?

Some 800 kids, many of them abused, disabled, or in need of help of some kind, have been using the facilities every year recently. Some have come from as far as South Wales and many stay on to fish for three or four days at a time. When they stay on, Les is there to help them with swim preparation and tackle adjustments. The little water is prolific but it needs a little understanding.

The Metropolitan Police involved themselves in a scheme under the guidance of Les Webber recently. The idea was that a number of officers should each take a youngster under their supervision and teach them, not only to fish but to begin to understand the outdoors in general. Martin Founds of Anglers' World Holidays presented fishing holidays in Ireland for the winners of a light-hearted knock-out match recently. The final was held on Les's water and the prizes included the two junior winners and their officer "minders". It was my privilege to present the prizes on the final day and it was interesting to hear comments from the officers concerned. "My kid's doing well. I hope he wins. I've never been to Ireland ..."

All great stuff and part of a wonderful build-up of confidence in the Met. A means of developing an ongoing friendship between under-privileged kids and those who stand for law and order. Holidays in Ireland were surely deserved by those officers who sought to *prevent* crime by giving up some of their spare time. A worthy cause and a suitable reward, one might have assumed.

Alas, the officers were refused permission by their superiors, and the whole scheme was almost ruined overnight. Time was short. Passages had been booked. Kids were overjoyed at their prospects. How could they be told that their venture had been cancelled?

The truth, of course, is that they could not! Les, at almost a moment's notice, gave up a week's business, delegated some of his duties, and escorted the kids himself. On the face of it perhaps it was no great hardship and it is possible that any one of us might have jumped at the chance, but life is seldom all that easy!

Les Webber and Angling Projects will probably always be seeking more money for courses of tuition, more money for prizes and materials, and for equipment still needed to maintain the fishery that gives the kids a break.

I spent a week in Canada fishing the Red River in Les's company. We enjoyed fish-fries and barbecues, boat rides and bank swims along with the incredible carp and catfishing on offer at that special venue. We could have caught more. We could have flogged away in the numbers or weight game, but we had no heart for either.

74

Instead we discussed the possibility of the next Gentleman's Occasion on the banks of his little lake and the chances of "cooking-up" some more money for the next batch of kids heading his way.

Les Webber is a good man who is now near to realising the dream of a lifetime and I, for one, am pledged to help in any way I can!

Chris Tarrant, Les's biggest supporter and close friend, is similarly pledged. Between us, and with the help of the fantastic "Team", we have raised over £18,000 for the Project *and* other charities. Les and Chris decided, at the outset of our special "cookout occasions", to split the "profits" with other nominated deserving causes. Les has divided out the shares, almost to the last penny, every year since and our agreement is that this is how it will remain.

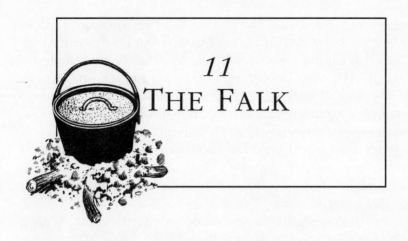

11
THE FALK

It was a dark, cold, winter's night in the early 1960s when a tall stranger came to my door.

"Fred Taylor?" he asked. "I'm Hugh Falkus. Just passing through and thought I'd call in."

I was taken totally off my guard but, at the same time, I felt nervously delighted. Here was someone whose skills and writings I had long admired. For him to come calling was a dream come true.

Hugh and I had corresponded occasionally in the past, and I had sought his advice on odd occasions but we had never met or talked on the telephone.

Hugh was "fed and watered" and urged to stay the night instead of pressing on to his destination. That, undoubtedly, was the start of our friendship, which lasted over 35 years.

On my way back from Scotland some years later, I called to see him at his cottage near Ravenglass in Cumbria. I had some fishing tackle with me since I had been seeking the perch of Loch Ken with some young friends, but I had no thoughts of fishing for trout or sea trout. I was a simple coarse fisher and, although I had some slight experience with a fly rod, I had not even considered the possibility of game fishing. Nor had I anticipated staying overnight. As it happened, however, I was to be given a special chance.

The river was low and clear. Fly fishing, although not total-ly a waste of time, was not offering much in the way of

opportunity but I was allowed to fish the worm from darkness until dawn. At first I was reluctant, but Hugh assured me
that a fish caught on a fly was just as dead as one caught on
a worm. The object of fishing a sea trout run, he said, was to
reap a natural harvest in a sporting fashion and there was
nothing unsporting about worm-fishing. It was, in fact,
requiring of as much skill as fly fishing.

From then on I was hooked upon sea trout fishing. I
caught my share when the chips were down and I spent
many nights alone on that lovely little River Esk praying for
the dawn not to come.

I am not normally happy alone in the darkness. With a
good friend, I revel in night fishing; alone, I find it somewhat
scary! Laugh as much as you like; the hours of darkness can
do things to a person who is totally alone. It was not so on
the River Esk.

I felt comfortable and my concentration upon the job in
hand, which was to catch sea trout, never wavered. I loved
every precious minute of it and I knew that Hugh was right
when he called it a "friendly little river". I caught my first bag
of sea trout that night. I enjoyed fishing there alone but I felt
the need to share it with someone. I asked if I might possibly come again and was told that, of course, I might. Any
time!

When I first went back it was with thoughts of sea trout in
mind.

To be invited to fish the lovely little River Esk as a guest of
the great man was a privilege not extended to many people.
Most of the regular visitors to his cottage were fly fishers who
regarded themselves as his friends. I was a humble coarse
fisher who would never be able to claim such a relationship.
Or so I thought. I quickly learned how totally wrong I was
and how easy it is to misjudge the character of the special
people in one's life.

Hugh showed me a pool containing possibly 200 sea trout.
The water was low and clear. We kept our heads below the
level of the bank herbage and watched the restless fish.

"These are not the best of conditions but you might catch

one or two on a worm tonight," he said. *Again*, in the presence of skilful fly fishers, I was reluctant.

"Would that not be looked upon as an unsporting method?" I asked.

Hugh snorted. "There is no such thing as an unsporting method, nor is there an item of equipment that may be labelled unsporting. Only the person using it can be unsporting!" I have never forgotten those words.

It so happened that the worm outfished the fly on that occasion but I was never in any doubt about Hugh's brilliance with a fly rod. I learned to fly fish but never to compete.

In later years Hugh would join me and give me a lesson in fly fishing. I remember some of those nights with great joy. One, in particular, when Hugh instructed me to bring only my fly rods.

"Bring a floating line and a sinking line," he counselled. "If you want to fish the worm you can do it with your fly rod."

I should have known better!

In theory, such a procedure was possible but, in practice, I simply could not reach the spot where my instinct told me the fish ought to be.

It was a very frustrating time for me, particularly so as Hugh caught several nice sea trout on fly. I sat down in despair and cursed him for talking me out of bringing my bait rod with me. He laughed loud and long at my predicament. He knew I could only swing my tackle out lightly because of the worm attachment. Any attempt to fly-cast correctly flicked it off.

"I'm not laughing *at* you," said Hugh. "I'm laughing *with* you."

And, after a nip or two of Scotch, we both laughed with each other.

We relived the experience many times. Not all of sea trout fishing was deadly serious!

In later years, I introduced my brother Ken to the delights of Esk sea trout fishing. He loved every magic moment of those dark hours we spent together, and he was quick to learn. Quick also to endear himself to Hugh, who swiftly noted his ability as a practical and dedicated angler. He encouraged us both to fish hard and never to accept defeat.

The accepted rule at Hugh's lovely Cragg Cottage was that anyone who caught a 5lb sea trout should provide champagne for the next evening.

I caught one weighing 5lb 14oz and happily agreed. Ken caught one exactly one pound less and our earlier hopes of the extra celebration were dashed when Hugh declared Ken's fish to be below par.

"I *did* try," he assured me. "But my scales were too accurate to allow serious cheating!"

I later introduced Fred Buller to Hugh and I take credit for having done so. Their relationship was somewhat stormy (understandable when two perfectionists get together to write a classic work on angling in general) but it was nevertheless unique. Their combined efforts produced *Falkus and Buller's Freshwater Fishing* which, despite being ridiculed by a mini-minority, whose expertise ended at the number of split shots needed to cock a waggler match float, has stood the test of time, has been reprinted and reissued for the benefit of those who love fishing *and* who have the intelligence to appreciate superb writing!

There came a time when Fred Buller joined Ken and me at Cragg. Fred stayed with Hugh in the cottage; Ken and I shared the caravan on the hillside. We had in our possession a pair of walkie-talkies and we left one with Hugh and Fred while we went fishing with the other.

Two other guests arrived at the cottage and a four-sided poker game started around a bottle of Scotch. Ken and I fished for little reward until the heavens opened.

Should we quit there and then? I asked Hugh on the radio.

"No. No," he advised. "Carry on. You have the whole river to yourselves."

Didn't we know it!

An hour later we were wet, cold and thoroughly miserable.

"Persist. Persist," came the message from the cosy cottage. "Take shelter at Hazel Dub for a while and then proceed to Knott End."

An hour later there was no reply from the cottage. The radio lay crackling in the corner by the fireplace. Our messages were ignored or not even noticed as the next bottle was started! Meanwhile it rained! Harder, colder and faster. Ken and I retired to the caravan, dried ourselves off and opened our own bottle. I never told Hugh, but our toast that early morning was simply "To Hell with Falk, *and* his bloody sea trout." Enough was enough!

We did not receive, nor did we expect to receive, any sympathy for our naivety!

In recent years it has been my pleasure, helped by Alec Martin, to rustle up an outdoor campfire meal for Hugh and Kathleen, Bill and Marie Arnold (their close friends) and a few other local guests. The numbers have grown as the years have passed but it has always been a pleasant duty.

I introduced Alec because he was a fellow camper/outdoorsman/angler/harvester and I felt that he and Hugh should meet. They met and Hugh encouraged us to fish. We were inspired to fish certain pools by day but given sound advice about our night-time exploits. Alec succeeded brother Ken. His acceptance of the unique opportunities on offer amounted to gracious approval and another convert was born.

"Wait until you are absolutely certain that it is dark enough before you even *think* about fishing," said Hugh. "Then wait *another* half an hour!"

It would have been approaching midnight by then and I doubt very much if we were ever able to wait that long before fishing but the advice was sound. We caught our fair share of sea trout and herling and, acting upon Hugh's advice, we exploited the tiny becks by day while the main river was left to recover. There were, however, other experiences to be shared.

The account of how Hugh, from a vantage point up on a high bank, watched a salmon toying with a worm on the end of my line, however, has been brilliantly recorded in that section of his book *Salmon Fishing* which has to do with taking behaviour. The salmon played games with us both and, although I was dependent upon Hugh's commentary for information (he could see the fish; I could not), I found the experience fascinating. Frustrating but fascinating. The salmon actually had the worm in its open mouth and yet at no time could I possibly have set the hook.

Occasionally Alex and I would persuade Hugh to read the entire account from his book. We would listen enthralled at his total professionalism and I am thrilled to have been present during those unique moments.

Memories of actual facts become vague as the years pass and, while I recall many hilarious exploits in that lovely little valley, I can only remember fishing the whole night through with Hugh on one very special occasion.

I recall it because I was given a lesson in fly-fishing for sea trout by the master. I caught some fish myself, it's true, but the heavier bag by far was carried by Hugh as we walked across the swing bridge in the early morning.

It had been a night of action followed by one of those bonus dawn periods referred to by Hugh as "extra time". During the dark hours we had indulged in a little Scotch, we had had a few laughs, and now thoughts of hot tea up at the cottage were foremost in our minds. Hugh put away the fish, brewed a big pot of tea, and poured two cups. He laced each cup with a generous measure of Scotch.

"After such a night, we are deserving of a cup of Cragg tea," he announced. I agreed. I drank mine, declared it to be sheer nectar, and Hugh poured some more.

Time passed. Conversation improved and increased. The level of the bottle slithered deliriously downwards!

Eventually Hugh exerted his authority. "You must get to bed, my dear chap," he said. "You'll be fit for nothing otherwise. Go now and get a good night's sleep!"

I looked at my watch as I went and, if my hazy memory is not at fault, it was precisely 11 a.m.!

Those were gloriously wonderful days. And nights!

There was more to our Cumbrian exploits than sea trout cleverly caught and flies expertly presented. There was an atmosphere that took us back to our childhood days and I have given thanks for that ever since!

The tiny becks that ran down the hillsides locally were not exactly stuffed with small brown trout but Hugh encouraged us to fish with fly rod tops and small red worms during our daylight hours. We agreed that it made no sense at all to disturb the river by day and we enjoyed many a breakfast of troutlets and bacon following Hugh's advice.

We scrambled up and down the rocky, overgrown slopes to extract a fish here and there with our improvised, so-called Falkus Rigs. It was an exhausting experience but the rewards were truly great.

As the years pass, I have found the going tough. The hills seem steeper, the fish fewer and the days shorter. My love of the outdoors has never waned, however, and I still regard the campfire meals I prepare in Cumbria as very special occasions. They began when Alec Martin, who joined me on one of my trips, wanted to say a special "thank you" to our hosts. Could we take them out to dinner one night? Or could we not entertain them out of doors in the area they loved so well?

So began what became known as the "Bonfire Feast".

"When are you coming up to light your bonfire?" Hugh would ask. And the date was usually fixed.

My protests that the affair had to do with campfires and *not* bonfires went unheeded but this cook-out became a regular feature on our summer calendar.

In the early days, Hugh and Kathleen with Bill and Mary Arnold (friends from nearby) were our only guests but, as time passed, more people began to turn up as the word was spread. It was almost as easy to cook for fourteen as for four, and when several of Kathleen's blackcurrant pies and a small ocean of cream followed the game casseroles generally on offer, life in the Cumbrian outdoors was recognised as being rather special.

Meal-time became memory time as Hugh and I recalled past events with great pleasure.

When Hugh learned that the end, for him, was near, he stubbornly refused to quit! He informed those around him that he fancied oysters and champagne, and they came in abundance. Oysters by the dozen; champagne by the buck-etful! Despite pain and disability, he lived his remaining days and nights to the full.

"Tell all my friends to have a drink on me when I'm gone," he instructed. "I want everyone to have a party and I'll make sure there's champagne for everyone." Hugh died on 30th March at midnight and he was true to his word. On April 14th a hundred or so people, from all walks of life, gathered around the Esk pool known as Meadow Dub. A tractor and trailer loaded down with ice and champagne arrived and, with due ceremony, corks were popped to the memory of a very special person.

Hugh wanted no sadness on the occasion but it was there despite the many smiling faces. He was missed then. He will be missed for a long time, and he will always be a part of angling's history.

My memories remain. My instructions are to continue the annual "Bonfire Feast" for as long as I am able and, God will-ing, I will do just that.

I doubt, however, that it will ever be quite the same.

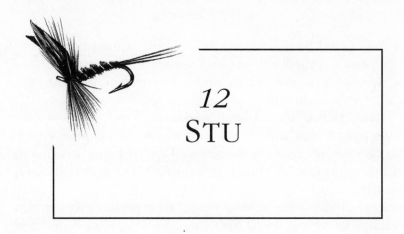

12
STU

I first met Stuart McKay in Winnipeg, Manitoba, and it turned out to be a very memorable occasion. There was also a totally coincidental bonus attached to it.

I had joined Martin Founds of Anglers' World Holidays on a trip to Canada to seek big lake trout, grayling, catfish and carp. Canadian Airlines had delivered us luxuriously to Winnipeg, where we had arranged to meet one Stuart McKay. He was to be our guide and host for the final week of our tour and this initial contact was to be a brief introduction.

There can be no doubt about Stu's Scottish ancestry. With a name like that his roots are obvious but somehow or other he does not look at all Scottish. He looks very Indian and, in fact, several generations back, a mixed marriage took place between Indian and Scot. Stu is rather proud of that fact and certain aspects of his hunter/conservationist philosophy tend to prove that is so.

We met to enjoy a glass of wine together and to discuss what we would do when we met up again in two weeks' time, but Stu was anxious to pass on a message from 600 miles south – in the USA.

"I was talking to an old friend of yours last weekend," he said. "A guy named Dan Gapen – who is also a good friend of mine. Do you know him?"

Dan and I had fished together in places as far apart as Arkansas and Canada's Ogoki wilderness area and of course

I remembered him. However, it had been a long time.

Stu and I immediately had something in common.

"He says he's going to try and come up when you're here next month," said Stu.

"That," I said, "would really make my day."

We parted company then and it was some eight days later that Stu met us again at Winnipeg Airport. I was anxious to go fishing in the Red River and I asked him if he had seen any carp.

"Holy shiner – minnows, Fred," he replied. "I've got 'em feeding out of my hand! You can damn near walk on their backs downstream and they've been eating three buckets of corn a day on your instructions!"

I wanted to get started at once the following morning but Stu insisted that first I caught a "pussie cat" (his affectionate nickname for channel cat).

I had caught channel catfish before but none as big as those reported to be prolific in the Red River at Lockport. I looked over the immaculate cabin that was to be our home for the next eight days and marvelled at how several anglers had made it look like a bomb crater within minutes! It was always so. It will always be so. When anglers dump their gear and start to talk fishing, a "suite" becomes a "tip" very quickly and all good operators and outfitters accept it as the norm.

A voice behind me said, "I'm your guide for this week and you'll do what I tell you to do!"

My reactions were immediate. For the briefest of moments I wondered if this domineering person was for real but then came the flash of recognition. Dan's voice – from all those years back. Old 'moose-loose-in-the-boat" as I had once called him as he mangled everything in sight under his feet to grab a camera or some other item of equipment. We shook hands, embraced (in manly fashion!) and Stu remarked that he guessed we two did indeed know each other!

The sad part was that Dan and I could not fish together once more since he was running a tight schedule and had taken a special and lengthy side-step to join us briefly. We had to part next day.

I caught three catfish under Stu's guidance. The first was a fish of 21lb which took a chunk of cut bait and put me on the trophy list since it was just long enough to qualify. It was an also-ran compared with some of the 30-plus pounders caught later by other members of the party but it suited me. The other two were "double digits" – about 15lb each.

Stu kept me going with portions cut from goldeye bait fishes and assured me that he would back fresh fish baits against traditional chicken liver and stinkbaits at any time of the season. His results appear to support his claims.

There is no doubt whatsoever that Stu is a catfish expert on his own home ground. He is bold enough to *guarantee* a catch *and* smart enough to honour it. He understands catfish and he pays them the same respect as we are apt to pay our own carp, but he confessed to me that he was at times bored with the same old routine.

Being with him in a boat, to face the tumbling waters of the dam, to feel the almighty tug of a big cat in deep water was a thrill. Doing battle with those great, bewhiskered bundles of bone and muscle gave me great satisfaction.

"If you do it almost every day, you have to go on auto-pilot or it would drive you mad," said Stu. I think I understood.

"That's why I want to get into these carp more," he continued. "Hell, we've got an amenity here that's untouched, unexplored and unexploited. No-one has any respect for carp but no-one understands them either. I'm beginning to know a bit more about them and I'm totally amazed at their power. I've caught one or two since you guys got me all worked up about them but I sure as hell have a lot to learn."

It has to be said that Stu was quick to learn. He fell in love with long rods, became fascinated with float tackles, drooled over electronic bite alarms, and finally became convinced that No. 4 hooks were quite large! He had been using cod hooks! Obscene hooking things, but best in the circumstances for giant catfish.

Getting to know Stu was a privilege. I learned a great deal from him. I am quite sure he learned a little from me. One thing we found out together was that if you choose a spot on the Red River system, where shallows run into deeps (and that means just about anywhere!), and bait it up overnight, you will catch carp there next morning! Most of them will be "double-digits" – about 10 per cent of them (by my own experiences) will be over 20lb, and 40-pounders are certainly there for the catching. We learned together that float fishing was as good a way of catching carp as any – and that sophisticated baits, rigs and bite indicators were surplus to requirements! Soaked corn for "chum" (as the Canadians refer to groundbait) plus sweetcorn and bread hookbaits were all our party needed to catch well over a ton of carp!

Stu, it seems, has been responsible for the conservation of channel catfish in that particular stretch of the Red River. He has promoted barbless hooks (now mandatory in Manitoba) and a catch-and-release policy regarding fish over a certain size. Generally speaking he is seeing his policies come to fruition. Most anglers now return their catches at once. Those who enjoy catfish to eat are happy to retain the smaller and more edible specimens.

There are, however, a few visitors from the USA determined to take away great cooler boxes full of fish. "Holy shiners, Fred," said an outraged Stu one afternoon when a boat pulled in with four massive, double-figure catfish kicking out their last breaths against the bottom. "What the hell would anyone do with 60lb of catfish meat? If they do that every day for a week, how much of it is going to be fit to eat by the time they get home?"

Clients are clients when you are in the boat-hire and guiding business but, to Stu's credit, he allowed his heart to rule his head in the circumstances.

"I need clients," he said "but I can do without that sort!"

I feel obliged to admire that kind of attitude!

There came a time, in the midst of all the excitement and laid-back fishing, when the urge to see more of that great water system overtook the desire to catch carp, and Stu took several of our party on an exploratory trip.

The Red River, from the dam to Lake Winnipeg, is about 30 miles long. Every twenty or so yards is a brand new carp swim

that only needs an overnight baiting with soaked corn to produce. You could fish a different spot every day for ten seasons and never visit the same place twice! There seems to be no limit to what can be expected in terms of angling amenities. The so-called Netley Marsh, between the dam and Lake Winnipeg, has *180 square miles* of channels, lakes, reeds and rush beds. It has shallows and deeps, and it opens out into areas of water that could embrace a hundred British reservoirs. It is said that you could walk across the backs of spawning carp there at any time during the spawning season! I believe those who say so!

It took me a few days to realise that this Red River was the same Red River that I had fished on the Minnesota/North Dakota border in the USA many years ago with my friend Jack Vasconcellos. Stu pointed out features and explained the geography.

Here, he suggested, was the greatest unexplored amenity

the Province of Manitoba could offer to the rest of the world.

I fished for part of the time with Bill Chisholm, a visiting British angler, and Dennis Maiskymetz of the Manitoba Tourist Authority. At one stage, Dennis and Bill decided that a cold six-pack of beer and some burger sandwiches would be in order, and left me in charge of the outfits while they went to collect the same.

It goes without saying that I hooked my best fish of the week while they were absent.

I had become well used to landing my own fish in the oversized tea-strainer that Canadians referred to as a "dip-net" but, after a time, I realised that this was not going to be quite as easy as I thought. It was a big fish. Big enough and strong enough at least to cause me problems.

I have no idea how long it took me to land it. All I know is that my arms were about to fall off and that I had the wretched thing to the net a dozen times before I finally got it to fold up and become enmeshed. As I did so, I was suddenly aware of a round of applause! A couple of anglers on the far bank and half a dozen spectators on the bridge upstream had witnessed the whole episode and had spontaneously given their approval. An old ego sailed right to the top of the mast as a result of such appreciation!

That fished weighed 24lb. It was an immaculate, beautifully coloured, fully scaled common carp and if I never see a bigger or a more handsome fish I shall not be over-concerned. My two companions came back in time to see it released and to pour me a well-earned cooler! From that spot Bill and I caught 37 carp, including two 20-pounders, in two five-hour-long sessions.

As I packed to leave Canada on that occasion I was conscious of a hint of doubt. Would carp fishing, or indeed any other kind of fishing in the UK, ever be the same again!

When seven anglers, not really trying very hard, can total up over 300 carp, mostly into double figures and including 34 (by my reckoning) over 20lb, the fishery has to be regarded as something *very, very special*. I said as much to Stu as I prepared to depart. "God willing, I will be back," I assured him.

"Well," he said, "we're going on an eight-day deer hunt in late October. It will be rugged out there in the bush. Cold as a well-digger's butt, but we'll have a good campfire going and you're welcome to join us if you wish."

"OK," I said. "I'll come and be camp cook."

I don't know why I said it and anyway I figured no-one would think any more of it, but I was wrong. Letters from Stu on my return to England convinced me that he had taken me at my word and that I was, indeed, expected to go. I needed no arm-twisting and a very understanding wife gave me her blessing. So I went.

There was a fine layer of snow on the ground as we loaded the truck and boat trailer for the 100-mile journey east. It had cleared a little as we took the first boat-load of gear across the Winnipeg River. The sun came through briefly as we unshipped the final load and pitched camp. A 16' x 10' tent housed our bedrolls and clothing; the rest of the gear was placed around the camp in weatherproof boxes.

We had essentials like flour, baking powder, salt, bacon, tea and eggs. We also had reserves of beans, soup and other tinned food. The object, however, was to eat wild food for much of the time. In that respect we were extremely fortunate.

Stu, I learned, is a bow hunter. His expertise with a traditional long-bow has to be seen to be believed. Not for him the compound "wheely" bow. His bow is similar to those used by the British bowmen of old except that, to use his own words, his has "only a 100lb pull".

Those old warriors, he told me, were trained to shoot a required number of arrows every day from bows with pulls of 120lb! He is indeed well-read regarding British history! He can also shoot! His friend Pete McKenzie, who joined us, is a fine shot with both rifle and shotgun. At target practice, I "passed muster" but my main interest lay in the camp-cooking allied to some very laid-back pike fishing.

Our camp was close to the water on the banks of a secluded bay. We were, as far as I could tell, the only folk around for many miles. It took a few hours and an overnight, jet-lagged sleep for me to get my act together but, while the hunters planned their strategy, I prepared meals and enjoyed my pike fishing. An "optonic" bite alarm warned me when my dead bait was taken and after a couple of abortive "runs" I caught a pike weighing about 11lb. The first of the wild food and only one of many during the eight day stint, Stu returned on the second day with a squirrel and ruffed grouse, both shot with his long bow. Pete pulled down a Canada goose with his 10-bore and a cartridge loaded with monstrous, steel, BB shot. Later they produced another grouse and a fat mallard. All told, the larder was extremely well-stocked within the first few days and we were somewhat spoiled for choice of meals.

Having hit a squirrel and a grouse, Stu, unbelievably, missed his first shot at a small deer. He "scraped" it, he claimed, after trying to make up his mind whether we needed the meat all that badly. It mattered little. We were in good shape.

On the third day we were visited by the grey jays or, as they are referred to in Manitoba, the "Whisky Jacks". These are not as brilliantly coloured as the blue jays of the American continent but their markings are far from dingy. They are very adept "scroungers" and quickly learn that they are welcome in most camp sites. One of our own particular visitors was smaller, slightly more aggressive, and certainly tamer than his colleagues. He would almost, but not quite, take food from an extended hand. My friends decided to call him Fred! (Fred Jay in case you don't get the point.)

Pete daily ran amok with the small chain saw and kept me well-supplied with firewood. Pine burns quickly and produces little in the way of coals but, by using big logs and packing them tightly, we kept the frost at bay overnight. A kick or two in the early dawn rejuvenated the flames and within minutes the black billy was on the boil with life-restoring tea.

Life in a winter camp can be full of surprises. I was alone and busy with the Dutch oven one day when I was suddenly aware of an orange-clad black-powder hunter at my side.

92

He was, he said, camped a mile or two away and had smelt the wood smoke. I had not heard as much as a cracked twig – so silent had been his approach, and I was impressed.

It had to be that way on a deer hunt, he assured me, and after a bit of practice I found out that I, too, could handle the soundless approach. Whether I could have kept an eye open for deer signs at the same time remains in doubt.

I enjoyed my time in that remote camp. I felt I was in a totally magical world and, on reflection, I suppose I was.

Thoughts of killing a deer with a broad-head arrow gave me cause for concern. It would not have suited me to partic-ipate and I questioned the morality of the kind of death inflicted by such methods. It had to be slow. Did it not? The animal could not die an instant death as it would when struck by a high-velocity bullet. Could it? It had to be tracked down by the trail it left behind as it bled to death. Was that not so?

I had asked all these questions in advance and they had been answered to my satisfaction.

In order to kill a deer with a bow, it is essential to be very close to it. That not only demands great skill but it also ensures accurate shooting. Death is not instantaneous but my hunting friends convinced me that it *is* quietly dignified. Stu told me that he once put a broad-head through a deer and that it actually carried on browsing for a few seconds before collapsing and dying on the spot.

I was further convinced when both he and Pete dragged in a fine buck on the last morning. The arrow had passed through its neck. It had been fired from only a few feet away and had been deadly accurate.

On that morning our breakfast consisted of deer liver and onions, kidneys, bacon and grouse breasts. A slight improve-ment on tradition!

It was a fitting end to a very special occasion and as we loaded up the boat for the final crossing, a few white flakes mingled with the swirling, steamy ashes of the now fully doused and dormant campfire.

That was the first of many wilderness camps with Stu. Annually our numbers grew and we eventually speculated on a big canvas tent with a wood-burning stove facility. I remember all the camps well but there is one that I will remember above all others.

My arm had, somehow or other, found its way outside the goose-down sleeping bag and it was uncomfortably cold. I drew it back and shivered as I put it inside my track suit "pyjama" top to warm up in my natural body heat. Inside the bag I felt comfortably warm but two numb ears gave me cause to wonder just how cold it was in the outer darkness.

I switched on my tiny torch. The tent thermometer showed minus 15° Celsius and I wondered what I was doing in this Manitoba wilderness in such circumstances.

I shone the torch upwards and a million fairy lights twinkled back at me from the slightly sagging canvas. Miniature icicles, beads of pure ice, the end product of condensation caused by the breath of six sleeping bodies, verified the extreme conditions of this particular camp! It sounds somewhat sadistic but, in fact, it was more or less par for the course. Sleeping in a cold tent in a quality bag is not terribly fearsome. *Climbing out* is what takes the courage!

Stu, in the next cot, groaned. "Lord, I'm cold," he said. "What's it like outside?"

"Colder than in here," I responded.

He sat up, pulled on an extra sweater and tugged on his arctic boots.

"We need warmth," he counselled. "If we don't warm up we'll be done."

I could only conclude that his sleeping bag was not really up to handling the present sub-zero temperatures.

I bit the bullet and climbed out into the darkness. The embers of the outside campfire were still glowing and we kicked them to renew the flames. Firewood was stacked close by and we fed the flames until they leapt in the darkness to reveal the frost-spangled pines.

My watch said it was 2.30 a.m. I sat on a log and lowered the black billycan into the flames. Its overnight water content was covered with half an inch of ice but it surrendered to the blaze and was soon boiling. A carefully measured handful of

94

leaves went into it and tea, hot as fire and black as night, soon filled two enamel mugs. We cupped our hands around them, revelling in the extra warmth and, having savoured the magic brew, set about relighting the tent's small wood stove.

Wonderful things, these stoves. The chimney passes through an asbestos-lined hole in the tent wall and within minutes the whole interior is warm. Sometimes uncomfortably so. There is an arrangement of dampers which, supposedly, shuts down the fire and slows the rate of burning, but ours always has a habit of turning to ash within an hour. This means, of course, that we retire pleasantly warm but have to face a very cold world at dawn.

Soon smoke was pouring from the stack and those inside the tent were complaining about the heat! It is hard to please some folk! By now all thoughts of sleep had left me and I decided to sit out until dawn. Stu poured more tea, and laced it this time with a little rye whisky. Soon we were listening to the gentle, and not too gentle, snores coming from the tent.

"Look behind you, Fred," said Stu some time later. I turned to see dancing green and white lights in the dark sky over the bay. The Northern Lights were showing yet again for my benefit. Not as spectacular this time as on previous occasions but still breathtakingly beautiful against the pinewood foreground. I have listened to several explanations regarding the cause of the aurora borealis but, to tell the truth, I really do not care much one way or the other about the origins. I give thanks for the privilege of being able to see them occasionally in the cold night skies of Canada. On this very special occasion, however, there was more to come.

Suddenly, from the depths of the forest, came the sound of timber wolves calling. And from across the water came the reply of another pack. To say that they were howling would be to describe their calls unfairly. They were communicating in that fascinatingly eerie way so typical of those wild, woodland creatures. I have heard them before. I have heard the dingoes of Australia and the coyotes of the American West and always a tingle runs down my spine as I recall the words of an old friend from Idaho.

95

"They ain't howlin', Fred," he would say. "They's just a-talkin!"

We watched and listened for a while to our own exclusive "son et lumière" presentation. Who could deny that we were experiencing a sound and lights display not freely available to everyone? And who could deny that this was a particularly special privilege?

The sun rose slowly but with fiery brilliance across the water and those inside the tent began to stir. I put on another billy for their early morning tea. So passed yet another memorable night in the bush with a very special friend.

The next day we caught several small pike and feasted on fish and chips, at which point Stu declared our camp site would henceforth be known as Jackfish Bay. It has been so ever since and I sincerely hope that the Good Lord will allow me the privilege of one more "cold camp" visit.

13
CLANCY (AND BILL)

Strictly speaking, of course, his name is not Clancy but, since he is a horseman and a lover of the outdoors as well as an enthusiastic reader of the works of Banjo Paterson, I thought the name would suit him when I recorded our friendship some years ago. His (and my) friend's name is not Bill either but, for the purposes of this chapter they are to be known as Clancy and Bill. For the record, and just in case it is thought that there is mischief in my soul, I will tell you that their real names are Laurie and Bert. Two good friends; two frustrated bushmen. Frustrated because they are obliged to earn their livings amid the hustle and bustle of the "dusty, dirty city". In truth, Perth, Western Australia, is not particularly dusty or dirty, but that is how Paterson described the city in which he worked and where he dreamed up the character "Clancy of the Overflow". And those two close Australian friends surely grasp every opportunity of escaping from the city and hiding away in the bush or amid the sand dunes and beaches of the North.

I had met them both as a result of my interest in ferrets and shooting. Both were better shots than I am ever likely to be but they accepted me and made me welcome in their country.

When Clancy learned that I was interested in camping, rabbiting with ferrets, shooting, fishing, and generally on good terms with the outdoors, he and Bill invited me to join them on a long weekend trip. I remember it well because it was the first of many. I cannot recall the route we took but I remember that we had time to hunt for a few hours after we arrived at our venue. I remember, too, that first evening's camp and those that followed it.

The bushflies had retired for the day and their places had been taken by the ever-persistent "mozzies" of the Western Australian bush. The smoke from the campfire, generated deliberately, kept all but the most aggressive at bay and, as the light smoke wafted between us, Clancy ripped the tops off three cold beer cans. He passed one to Bill and the other to me.

"Who cares about city life?" he asked. "Who gives a damn about anything or anybody?" echoed Bill. I agreed. Out there in the bush country there was a serenity and a freedom which only those who have actually experienced it could begin to appreciate.

"Old Banjo Paterson might have been a city bushman," I said "but he really did have a feeling for the plains and the outback."

Bill took a pull from the cold "tinnie" and quoted: "He sees the vision splendid of the sunlight plains extended, and at night the wond'rous glory of the everlasting stars."

Emotional I may be and a softy at heart when it comes to the countryside, but I can never read or hear those words without a lump coming to my throat. I have, you see, been that route many times and it never ceases to thrill me.

Resting on the ashes of the fire was the big, black camp oven, known in other parts of the world as a Dutch oven, and the sweet smell of "damper" (soda bread more or less) filled the evening air. In another similar oven, rabbit portions sizzled alongside the onions and tomatoes picked freshly from the vine that morning. Pork slices mingled with the rabbit and a hint of fresh herbs added to the fragrance.

The rabbits had been shot earlier and had been dressed and cleaned in the waters of the creek. Jacket potatoes rested in their foil wrappings on the edge of the flame. There was plenty of time. Supper could wait for another hour and the meat would be all the more succulent for that. There was time, in fact, for Clancy and Bill to go off with the "spottie" to harvest tomorrow's rations. They plugged in the lamp, fired the motor, and were gone. I soaked a towel in water gathered from the creek, stripped off and washed away the trail dust and smoke for a fresh start to the night. In the light of the oil lantern I dressed out the remaining rabbits and put the portions briefly into salt water to clean. The ice bottles in the big cooler boxes (brought along for the purpose of keeping game fresh) supplied me with cold water for my generous measure of Scotch, and I put the dressed-out portions of meat into one of the boxes.

I heard a shot in the distance and the whine of a bullet across the open country. I caught a brief glimpse of the "spottie" beam above the brow of the hill and heard another shot, and another. Soon those two totally tireless hunting friends of mine would be back with yet another batch of "game" to be prepared. I put the blackened billy on to boil and lifted the lid off the camp oven to reveal a crisp, brown damper.

The billy came to the boil as the four-wheel-drive "ute" pulled up by the fire and Clancy began dressing out the still warm rabbits. I tipped in a measured handful of tea, let the billy boil again and saw the leaves surface and sink slowly to the bottom. Hot as fire, black as night and without milk or sugar, billy tea is the drink most appreciated in the bush country. Somehow it refreshes and cools despite its lip-searing heat. Its peculiar smoky flavour is rather special in the Australian outback.

The mozzies had now retired, the evening air was beginning to chill as we "dressed for dinner" by cleaning up with the same sodden towel and changing our shorts.

Hot damper, roast rabbit and jacket potatoes, eaten and relished in the light and warmth of the campfire, were appreciated by the whole crew, including the self-appointed cook. Tomorrow there was fresh liver and bacon and eggs for breakfast. With luck there would be freshly caught crayfish on the menu for supper.

I have always said that campfires encourage conversation. They perform their functions earlier in providing cooked food for hungry hunters but in the shadows and the reflections come memories of days past. Of limit bags achieved, of successes and failures, of truths and lies, of good times and bad times, but most of all of the deep friendship that only exists under exacting conditions. Good Scotch whisky diluted with water from the creek, or a sip or two of excellent Australian wine to accompany the superb after-dinner cheese, adds to the feeling of remoteness and friendship and, as sleeping bags are rolled out under the stars, a heady tiredness guarantees unbroken sleep until the dawn's chill brings wakefulness once more. Newspapers, telephones, watches, daily chores and routines are forgotten. It is impossible to believe that they ever existed. Life takes on a new meaning and there is a peace which demands a better pen than mine to describe.

Such was the first campfire I shared with Clancy and Bill. Around it we learned more about each other, established a friendship that was to last until this day, and was to be the forerunner of many other trips into the somewhat neglected areas of Western Australia. I remember them all but I recall one with special affection.

"You never did get around to having 'roo-tail stew last time you were here," said Clancy, "but you are going to experience that culinary delight before you leave this time. Take no notice of what people say, and use your own judgement. That's all I ask," he continued.

I had eaten kangaroo steaks the night before (unknown to him) and, since I had formed my own judgement on previous occasions, I had no fears as to what was in store for me.

"We will go," he said, "and do the job properly. Not for us the phoney Pommy survival practised by you and your cobbers in the UK. On this trip, if we don't catch fish or kill game, we will go hungry. No half-measures! We are going to do this as it should be done. You can bring flour, salt and tea, that's all. The rest is down to us. We'll get our own tucker or go hungry."

I put my rods together and rolled up a "swag" Aussie-style. A blackened billy, some dry tea, salt, a bag of flour and a sleeping bag, in which was secreted a bottle of good Scotch whisky (for snake bites and other emergencies!), completed my kit. I felt somewhat vulnerable and believed strongly that we should have taken some "insurance", at least in the form of bacon and beans. It was unheard of going bush without any real sustenance. But I was outvoted from the outset. Bill and Clancy turned up with the four-wheel-drive ute and a boat in tow. In the boat were beach rods, gill nets, rabbit traps, a rifle and a cooler box containing ice, fruit, vegetables and another bottle of emergency bush medicine.

"This," I said, "could hardly be regarded as a serious survival exercise. It is no different from the phoney Pommy ones you are at pains to slander." Those may not have been my exact words, but the meaning was clear!

I was told that man could not be expected to live on fruit or vegetables alone but that they could help to make freshly caught fish or game more palatable. I noted the Dutch camp oven in the back of the ute and figured that, if the worst came to the worst, we would not starve on billy tea and "damper"!

The temperature was exactly 86°F when we set off north from Yanchep and, as we travelled along the coast road, the mercury peaked at 100°F. The sea breeze had a cooling effect upon us but, when we turned off on to the direct though horrendous bush trail, the interior warmed up considerably. Even so, we were in good shape when we made camp some 125 miles later.

A lot had happened in between times, of course, and as the sun began to sink over the dunes I took the big axe and gathered firewood for the night.

"We need a strong swimmer to take out the gill net," said Bill. And Clancy echoed "Yes. A strong swimmer. I've got a bad back!"

It does not take a lot of figuring out who was pressed into volunteering, and a few moments later I was battling with the rollers trying hard to drag the leading end of the net with its buoy and anchor attachments 30 or 40 yards out into the

Indian Ocean. It was not a pretty sight. Nor was it a very successful venture.

I am no sea angler but I was prepared to believe that putting out a gill net at right-angles to the shore would produce enough food for breakfast. I struggled against the tide and wrestled with corks and leads in an attempt to make it all work, but I failed. There had been a blow a few days previously and the present north-wester was bringing in great rafts of seaweed. Within minutes the net was weighed down and I was under pressure to keep my head above water. For a time it was a stalemate situation but, in the end, I was obliged to submit. The water was warm and the exercise was pleasant enough, but there was no way I could win the battle.

We hauled in the net and tried, for the next half hour or so, to clear it of weed before stowing it in the boat once more. Even in that short and desperately inefficient session, however, there was one fish enmeshed. I've no idea what it was and it was not big enough to make much difference to our rations one way or another, but we kept it for the next day.

Meanwhile, Clancy had loaded the camp oven with onions, potatoes and kangaroo tail portions and it was simmering gently over the campfire as I began to rid myself of some of the salt and sand. The aroma of the stew wafted over the camp behind the great sand dunes. The north-west wind blew over our heads where we had settled on the sheltered side, and we listened to the pounding of the distant surf. It seemed strange that here we were protected when a few yards away the wind was stirring up the white sand and making life unpleasant.

"Do not try to be too technical about 'roo-tail stew," said Bill. "All you need are potatoes, onions and the 'roo-tail. A little water, pepper, salt and a goodly wallop of chilli will transform it into a meal fit for a king."

And, as the cold night air dried the sand and salt on my bare legs, I crawled nearer to the campfire in anticipation. I have cooked many campfire meals in my time. I have also been privileged to eat at the campfires of bushmen much more experienced than I, in other parts of the world, but I do not remember *enjoying* a campfire meal more than that great dish of 'roo-tail stew! Plenty have been as good but none better.

We crawled into our swags by the light of the lantern and, instead of counting sheep, I gazed upwards at the everlasting stars of the southern hemisphere before dropping into a sound and dreamless sleep. In the early hours of the morning the north-west wind began to gather strength and my sleeping bag began to "balloon" under its influence. The stars had disappeared. A few yards away, in strict competition with the wind, Clancy began to snore. Well, perhaps, not so much a snore as a vicious snarl that challenged every dingo, fox or wildcat in the vicinity to a duel to the death! It irritated me but I consoled myself by thinking that no man or beast would venture close enough to investigate the source!

Dawn came with a hint of rain and a further increase in the strength of the north-wester. I looked at my watch. It was 4.45 a.m. My sleeping bag was already damp with dew or falling rain. Bill was already up and moving.

The fire burst into flame under his expert coaxing and soon the billy was boiling. It is many years now since I first tasted black billy tea but I do not remember a more welcome cup.

I have to confess that the aroma of bacon and eggs would have added to its flavour on that morning but there was no time to consider the possibility of cooked food even had it been available. Totally exposed, with black clouds above and thunder rumbling in the distance, we stowed the gear. Last night's utensils had to be washed up and I gathered them and walked into the sea. There, with seaweed and sand, I scoured them spotless and rinsed them in the waves. The morning air was cold but the sea water was warm and it was not an unpleasant chore.

I scanned the beach for signs of others but it seemed we were the only humans around for many miles. Perhaps they already knew what we were beginning to fear ourselves. That this situation was not going to improve! In fact, as we pushed on farther north, it became considerably worse and by midday, after stopping off at several other bays and beaches, we were obliged to admit that this was no longer fun. Homesteads and civilised living were calling us and we headed south as the torrent increased.

So much for the romance of the bushland. What, I wondered, would Banjo Paterson have made of this lot?

Nevertheless it had been a good camp and a good experience. I would hate to have missed it but there were brief spells during it which I have no desire ever to repeat.

Clancy, Bill and I have shared many experiences since those early days. All have been associated with the gathering of wild harvests and a general love of the outdoors that is shared by us all. They all have to do with friendly conversation stimulated by a measure or two of superb Australian wine and a reluctance to return to the "foetid air and gritty of the dusty dirty city, (which) through the open windows floating spreads its foulness over all".

14
RALPH

His name is Ralph but he was once known to all as Bullock. One-time poacher, expert game shot and naturalist, this lively ex-pugilist was undoubtedly among the most knowledgeable of rabbit hunters in the country. It has been said that he had the ability to think like a rabbit, and the countless thousands he caught in a lifetime spent in their pursuit around the Vale of Aylesbury, where he was born, suggest that this is so.

Today, because rabbits have overcome the dreaded disease of myxomatosis and are now approaching plague proportions, the skills of the old rabbit hunters are proving invaluable to farmers and landowners. Vast areas of pasture and growing crops are laid bare each year, despoiled by the ravages of the ever-increasing number of rabbits. The outlawing of the cruel but deadly efficient gin trap in the 1950s has meant that their numbers are now more difficult than ever to control, and it is fortunate indeed that the crafts of the old-time hunters have not been lost. Long-netting at night, snaring and ferreting have now become respectable pursuits, and are the only means of rabbit control left other than humane traps and the administration of cyanide gas. Ralph still retains his remarkable rabbiting skills. He has lived long enough to pass them on to a younger generation who, in turn, will do the same. During the myxomatosis era, many of the old rabbit hunters died, and their secrets died with them. Ralph was among those who remained to bridge the gap.

It has been my privilege to shoot, snare, long-net and ferret with him over a long period. In my youth he taught me much of what I know of the game today and I have also, for the past 30 years, enjoyed the company of one of his much younger pupils. Malcolm Baldwin moves like a cat in the darkness, has an incredible sense of direction, and an ability to "smell out" rabbits. He learned his skills, as I did, from being allowed to accompany Ralph, to do as he was told and to be seen and not heard. Today he is a game shooter, rabbiter, deer stalker and naturalist of the highest degree.

Despite the all-out war waged against them, rabbits are still on the increase. They are experts at survival and it is necessary to know their lifestyle if they are to be reduced in number. Ralph is still as well-informed on that as ever and, like me, recalls the past with affection.

On a night as black as pitch, with no moon and only the slightest breeze, he and I took our long-net and swiftly and silently pegged it strategically across a field chosen in advance, with the breeze blowing *towards* the net, which was set on its ten or more 2'6" tall hazel stakes to its full length. Behind it lay the many holes of the hedgerow "bury" or burrow, which was home to the rabbits. They were feeding several hundred yards out in the field.

The net comprised two running lines of 100 yards each on which 150 yards of loose netting ran freely. Once the net was set, Ralph crouched behind it with a finger placed lightly on the taut top line.

I walked quietly around the perimeter hedge to the opposite end of the field. Then, quartering steadily, shaking a box of matches as I walked, I drove the outlying rabbits towards home and the unseen net. Ralph felt a rabbit immediately it hit the net and became ensnared. The "bagging" of the net slid along its top and bottom lines to prevent its escape. He instinctively knew whether to move left or right and, with no more than a quick twist of the fingers, dispatched the rabbit in the mesh. On a good night a dozen rabbits were shaken out of the net as it was picked up ready for the next "drop".

Today, at over 90 years old, he occasionally talks of our long-netting for the sheer sport of it, or as a favour to anxious farmer friends. During the Depression and the lean years of rationing after World War II, rabbit, hare, and other game served as food for meat-hungry families. He had no children of his own, but many neighbouring youngsters ate meat as a result of his rabbiting skills. "What good's a few penn'orth of meat to a growing kid?" he would ask. He was not, however, a benevolent benefactor. He charged a fair price for his game, but preferred to sell to individual families rather than to hotels and catering establishments, though he may well have made more money that way. His object was to break even on cartridges, bus fares, ferret food and nets. He almost certainly did better than that.

He was at his active peak before and during World War II when he was employed as a laundry machinist. The factory was used as a fire-watching base and, since he lived adjacent, he eventually found himself on permanent nightwatch duty. The hours he worked would be called "unsociable" today, but during the winter months they allowed him to work his ferrets several times a week. Today he loves to join me in the occasional hunt.

When the leaves have fallen from the hedgerows and the nettles have wilted, leaving the rabbit holes clearly visible, he will join me with purse nets, spade, probe and ferrets to an area checked in advance. Several days previously I may have been at work with secateurs cutting away brambles and briars to make the holes easier to net. He works silently and swiftly; he avoids walking on top of the burrow if it is at all possible.

He treads lightly lest his footfalls echo through the underground tunnels and give warning to the rabbits below. He spreads his purse nets over each hole in turn and pushes in their retaining pegs. He double checks to see that all holes are covered, and skirts the burrow to see that no tiny escape or "bolt" hole has been missed. Moving downwind and standing well back from the entrance holes, he slips in one, two, three or four loose jill (female) ferrets and allows them to hunt underground. Occasionally one or other of them will return, dislodge a net and dart back down into the darkness again. Ralph swiftly resets the net, and continues his silent vigil. Working with him on the opposite side of the hedgerow, I communicate by whistling quietly to attract his immediate attention. He may respond by snapping his fingers. A finger to the mouth indicates absolute silence, a shaking of the fist means that he has heard rabbits moving below ground. All the while he watches and listens, ready to pounce the moment a rabbit bolts.

Bumping noises below ground echo upwards, telling us that the ferrets have located their quarry and are forcing them to run. In their haste to escape, the rabbits stamp their hind legs in warning to others nearby and, if all has been done correctly, the exodus begins. A streak of brown fur leaves one of the holes, the net "purses" on its drawstring, and the rabbit is immediately enmeshed. Ralph grabs it, places his foot over the now uncovered hole to prevent any further escapes, dispatches it while it is still in the net, and covers the hole again with a new net from his pocket. "Always keep a couple of nets in your pocket, boy," he says. "Plenty of time to take out the dead rabbit *after* the hole's been reset." He straightens the temporarily discarded net, shakes out the rabbit and hangs it up nearby. All the time he watches and listens, and somehow or other almost invariably manages to position himself near to the hole chosen by subsequent escapees.

As the jill ferrets reappear, he picks them up and puts them into their carrying bag. In the event that a jill fails to reappear after half an hour, he announces that it is now time to "use the liner". He has no faith in electronics and the latest in transmitter collars does nothing to excite him. He believes in sending down a highly trained "little boy" to locate a "little girl". From another bag he produces a big hob (male) ferret, fits a collar and clips on six yards of line, which is marked at one yard intervals.

"A well-bred hob will always find a jill underground," he

says. "And when he does he'll kick her off the rabbit and take over from her."

It almost invariably works that way. Keeping the line nicely taut, but allowing it to run freely, he eases the hob into the hole nearest to where he heard the last sounds of action. The line fairly strips through his fingers as the hob runs on and, usually within minutes, the frustrated jill returns to his hand.

The hob, especially trained for the task, stays meanwhile with the rabbit, or rabbits. It is not unusual for several rabbits to be bunched up together in one dead-end situation.

Ralph pushes a flexible twig into the hole, finds the direction the liner has taken, and issues the command, "Dig here, boy." He seldom digs himself. "You want to learn, boy," he says. "You learn the way I did, the *hard* way."

Sometimes the going is tough, sometimes the holes are deep. Very often roots and rocks impede progress, but there is no easy way out of the situation. The liner has to be retrieved, and the only way to retrieve him is to dig to the end of the line. With good luck half a dozen rabbits could be the reward; with bad luck only a single, mangled carcase.

"In the old days," says Ralph, "we'd sometimes get a dozen or more at the end of a dig. I remember once getting two dozen."

Today, electronic homing devices are available for tracing the movements of ferrets underground but, although he agrees that they are excellent and reliable, Ralph prefers to use his eyes, ears and the sound judgement of his years of experience.

"I know we've got to keep the rabbits down," he says, "but we've still got to give 'em some sort of a sporting chance."

That about sums up the attitude of this old rabbiter. He is intolerant of mistakes and most of all those he makes himself, but he is basically a sportsman. When a rabbit seizes some unforeseen escape opportunity, he blames himself for missing it, but always he admires the rabbit for its cunning. "There'll always be some smarter than we are," he observes. "If there weren't we wouldn't have any rabbits left to catch.

109

And if the myxy' couldn't beat 'em there's no reason to believe we can."

When I was his young apprentice we would both eagerly await harvest time, when the combine ruthlessly hounded out those rabbits that had spent most of their time in the lush corn. Ralph would find out from farmers when certain fields were due to be cut and then locate any nearby burrows where disturbed rabbits would be likely to run.

With straw, hay, old sacking, turves and anything else available, we would block up the holes to an arm's length inside. Thus, when the rabbits sought sanctuary at top speed, they were only able to go in so far. Once in, they stayed put and, when it was all over, he and I would reach in to dispatch them one at a time. He always insisted that "a rabbit with a pulled neck is better than one full of shot". I have always agreed.

He still shoots extremely well with his old, immaculate sidelock, but prefers to eat rabbits that have not been shot.

I have known him set wire snares in the late afternoon and visit them an hour or two after darkness has fallen to claim his victims.

"Don't leave wires down all night, boy," he advises. "If you do, like as not you'll have a visit from Reynolds (a fox) and he'll leave you just the heads. If you *do* leave 'em down, stay with 'em. It's a tough game in winter, but that's the only way."

He still has an eye for the "jumps". These are the long-grassed spots in a run or track made by a particular rabbit. It is a fact that rabbits use their own runs, follow the same path, and make their outward and inward jumps in the same spots each night. Ralph's instructions on snaring are precise. "Set your wire across the jump, boy, peg it just one hand high and open it up big enough to put your fist through. Bury your wires in the dirt to take the shine off before you use 'em, and make sure you remember where you've put 'em when you do." His concern here is for cattle and other stock. A carelessly left snare can be lethal if it becomes wrapped around an animal's hoof or tongue, and he hammers this message home to all who ask his advice. He lives by the country code, shuts gates behind him, respects standing crops and leaves no litter. He is a considerate man in an inconsiderate world. He respects the quarry he seeks and the privilege of being allowed to seek it.

I could never claim that every single word of his teaching was strictly "gospel" but he undoubtedly taught me a great deal. More than that, he made me *think* and he taught me to be observant.

Since writing his chapter, Ralph has now totally retired. Sadly we have enjoyed our last hunt together but I remember those early learning days and the later, informative years with great pleasure. Ralph did not "know it all" but by Jove he knew a lot. Praise be, he was wise enough to pass his knowledge on to novices like me.

"Diggin' 'a 'ole"

Before I entered the forces, I was obliged to cycle about 7 miles to and from my outdoor job with a grand lady who owned a grand house in the country. It was a happy existence with absolutely no prospects but it allowed me access to various countryside activities. I often camped nearby and caught rabbits from a big warren to share with my equally enthusiastic friends. Those were, I have no doubt, some of the happiest days of my life.

There was a road worker whom I passed almost daily on my journeys and I actually envied him his job. He trimmed verges, cut grass, laid hedges, and did the many other tasks that fitted in with his daily routine. I never saw him when he was not busy, but I never saw him under supervision. He was his own man. A wise old countryman from whom I gleaned much knowledge. I always stopped to talk to him. He never stopped working but loved to talk.

One day I passed and he was standing waist deep in a trench, tossing out spadefuls of Bucks clay onto the verge.

My total lack of intelligence and/or wisdom is betrayed by my remark at the time, and I cringe every time I recall it.

"What be you at?" I asked, using his own particular Bucks phraseology. "Are you diggin' a 'ole?"

"Course I ain't," he replied. "If you 'ad 'alf a brain you'd know I was makin' a bloody 'eap!"

I was humbled then and I have been ever since, but I never forgot. And I hope I have passed some of the wisdom on for the benefit of others like me!

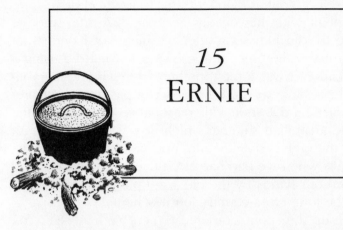

15
ERNIE

I met Ernie Chitty on my first visit to Australia in 1977. There
was no mistaking his total Aussie personality, and his love of
the outdoors was to be seen on his walnut skin. I had yet to
see a kangaroo and Ernie promised to take me next evening
to a spotting vantage point. Overnight, however, his 3,000
acre property was engulfed in a massive bush fire and when
he returned smoke-blackened and exhausted in the late afternoon, I abandoned all thoughts of the evening trip. Ernie,
however, had other ideas.

"She'll be right," he said. "A promise is a promise and we'll
go."

That established him immediately as my kind of man! He
had, he said, worn out two horses during the day's firefight-
ing but he'd be right after a shower and a clean-up.

We sat together in his hide and waited patiently for the
'roos to appear, but none did. It was a disappointment for me
but I got to know Ernie very well over a cold beer in the
nearby local club. On the way home with him I almost
wrecked my first Australian car when a very big 'roo jumped
out in front of me and ran up the headlights' beam. It was not
as I had planned it, but I was pleased to have satisfied my
desires.

That was the start of a long friendship with someone I
always regarded as a true Aussie gentleman. A sporting
gentleman, as I was destined to learn later.

He loved to go out at night with his four-wheel-drive "ute" to pot rabbits with his deadly accurate .22 rifle, and he invited me to join him soon after we met. Not having shot with a rifle for some time, and knowing I would be using a strange weapon, I was a bit apprehensive regarding my ability. I need not have worried. Ernie was a past master at presenting targets and I shot with reasonable accuracy. In the heat of the Australian summer's night it was essential to gut and clean the rabbits quickly and, not wishing to be greedy, I called quits when we had harvested five or six. We cleaned and washed our hands by the old wind pump and prepared to tackle the long cross-country journey home.

"Put one up the spout," ordered Ernie. "We may see a fox on the way back." I did as I was bid and stood ready in the back of the truck. What happened later was the first of many hilarious nights hunting rabbits by hand in the Australian bush. Ernie had said that we might "bamboozle" a few in the spot lamp and that it would not be too difficult to catch them. We had enough to eat, he told me, but we might get an odd bonus *without* bullets.

In shorts and sneakers, I chased rabbits in that deadly beam, and ripped my sunburned skin on brambles or briars (or the Aussie equivalent) grabbing at, and missing for the most part, those confused and bamboozled bunnies. It was hilarious. It was also exhausting. I know I caught several; I know I lost a great many more, but I do not remember a more exciting hunting exercise!

It was the first of many that I enjoyed with Ernie during the next fifteen years and, while I doubt if I will ever tackle such rigorous tasks again, I will remember them as highlights of my sporting life for ever.

It has always been my claim that I will never go hungry in a countryside environment. I would starve in the city but there is always food to be acquired in the country. The Western Australian countryside is harsh and seemingly sterile. Water is at a premium and I know from experience that I would be more likely to die from thirst than from hunger. Thoughts of being "bushed" without water still scare me and I have to thank Ernie for setting me straight in so many ways.

I spent almost five years in the western desert as a soldier, and I learned how to respect hostile environments during that time. I also developed a kind of love/hate/respect for wild and desolate places that obviously came through and was recognised by this grand old Australian. He talked calmly and logically about thirst, fire hazards and other dangers of the bush and outback. He told of how he had lived on kangaroo meat for weeks on end, and how he had survived many hardships in a hard and malevolent country. He talked of the old days when he rode fence lines, shot his food, baked his damper daily, and boiled his black billy every night before rolling out his swag under the stars. On the face of it, it sounded an idyllic existence but there were undertones of deprivation and despair that could not be ignored. Ernie was a harvester of food and I like to think that he recognised in me another soul with the same inborn instincts.

We shared many campfires together and we often talked on into the early morning about our hopes and fears. Always when we camped we tried to survive on what we were able to shoot or catch on rod and line. Our main source of supply was the rabbits, but we were able on occasions to take a small kangaroo.

On one occasion, Ernie suggested that we might well supplement our meat supplies with a few parrots. I had eaten them before and had, indeed, enjoyed them greatly.

Anyone who has tasted and approved of our native wood pigeon would certainly enjoy the very plentiful Australian green parrots. At that particular time, however, the shooting of parrots had been banned. I reminded Ernie of the fact and told him that parrots were now on the protected list.

"We'll take the bastards off it for this weekend," he said. "I've always made my own rules about what is or is not sacred and I know what I'm doing on my own property!"

I could not fault his thinking. He had never over-harvested any of his wildlife and there was never likely to be any shortage under his very conservation-minded management.

He had a hatred of foxes and feral cats because they were too numerous and because his stock had suffered from their predatory invasions. At night, whatever else he had in mind, there was always a preparedness for a meeting with "Charlie" (a popular name worldwide for the fox) – and he was merciless when one came within range of his high-powered rifle. He felt very much the same way with regard to feral cats!

Emus knocked down his fences so he shot emus in self-defence. His blue heeler dogs loved it when he did. The leg of an emu is about as big as a leg of lamb and Cooker and Pepper thought it was sheer bliss to be allowed to share one! Ernie was very wise in the ways of the Aborigines since he had shared their outback stations for many years. He had an uncanny sense of direction and was never lost or "bushed". He knew how to make fire without matches; he could find water in the most arid of conditions; but he never took the chance of not having a plentiful supply handy.

It was possible to live for weeks without food, he insisted, but you die very quickly without water. He could find food that would at least keep starvation at bay and he had no hesitation at eating the notorious wichety grubs so favoured by the Aborigines. He was challenged once to "put his money where his mouth was" by being offered a dollar for every wichety grub he would eat. One of Ernie's employees, well versed in the ways of the bush, went out and returned an hour or so later with a goodly supply gathered from the nearby blackboy trees.

"How do you want me to eat 'em?" asked Ernie. "Raw or cooked?"

He dropped a couple on the barbecue plate and devoured another couple raw! The challenger called off the bet, paid his dues and departed!

"The mongrel did me out of 25 bucks," Ernie complained as he left!

In a world where heat, dust and flies would deter many folk from venturing into the bush, I learned, with Ernie's guidance, to accept and even enjoy what was on offer. Where else in the world could I venture forth after dark in November dressed only in sneakers and shorts, to shoot rabbits in a "spotty" lamp? Where else could I work ferrets until darkness fell, light a fire to boil the billy, cook freshly dressed rabbits for supper, crawl into a sleeping bag under the stars, and be off with the ferrets again at crack of dawn? I would not want all my rabbiting to be along the same lines, but there was a certain magic in Ernie's company that defied description. I know I lack the knowledge and the experience of the true bushman but I am, at heart, a bushie. While certain Aussie friends of mine are happy to bounce around on ocean boats in search of fish, I revel in the discomfort of the bush. I have, if you like, learned not only to accept its challenge but to love it for what it is because of Ernie's influence. I respect a hostile environment and take no chances. I am no tracker but Ernie showed me, early in our relationship, how to read many of the elementary tracks of the bush. I know now when a tiger snake, a feral cat or a goanna has been down a rabbit hole, and I give that particular bury or warren a miss. I am not smart enough or experienced enough to know whether the creature is still present or not, but know enough not to look for trouble.

I once located and shot (well, another friend did the shooting) a big tiger snake on Ernie's property. It turned out that Ernie had located an even bigger one in the vicinity a few days previously and, being on horseback, had been obliged to dismount. In that area there are no trees or rocks. It is simply sand and scrub offering nothing in the way of a natural weapon. Ernie, dauntless or mad as a hatter, whichever way you care to interpret it, dispatched it with a stirrup iron in his clenched fist! Some knuckle duster! After 73 years in the bush, however, he probably knew more or less what was expected of him!

He tried to explain to me many times the laws of the Aboriginal tribes. He told of the "songlines", those ancient invisible tracks that were "sung" into being by the religious rituals followed by the native tribesmen. He told of some of the weird beliefs held by the Aboriginals, of their "dream times" and their spirits. I did not understand too much of what he said. Nor, perhaps, did he, because his explanations were vague. He did, however, conjure up visions of old Australia that were born of a true love of his country.

He told of the hard times, the days of the hungry and totally demoralised swagmen who came to beg food at sundown. He had known poverty himself and, although he administered rough justice to those who tried to take advantage of him, he showed great kindness to anyone genuinely in need.

He told me tales of his earlier bush existence and how he trapped rabbits, drove cattle and worked hard at any task to earn the money to exist. He took pride in the fact that he could always provide his family with food at any time of the year. Butchers' bills, he insisted, were unknown to him.

His wife Jess, who remains a dear friend of my family to this day, rode her horse and fed her children while in the saddle! They were indeed two of a kind.

I love the Australian climate but I do not have to work in it and I marvel at the spirit of those early settlers from whom Ernie and Jess were descended. While Ernie often told me of the hard times, Jess would sometimes recall the light-hearted occasions. She had shared his life for over 50 years!

Ernie was, perhaps, the equivalent of a British pot hunter and he insisted that the bushland would always provide for those who treated it with respect. When he and Jess ran a riding stable on one of their earlier properties it was their custom to offer lunch to some of their guests.

"Waste not; want not" was the doctrine they preached and they lived up to it.

Since Ernie was then in the farming business, it went without saying that he sold the best of whatever he produced and transformed that which was less saleable into food for the household. He would, for example, shoot a couple of kangaroos at the same time as a couple of old wethers, bone the whole lot out and put it all through the big mincer in the shearer's quarters. The resulting sausages, he said, were especially appreciated by his guests. Having tasted similar "snaggers" myself, I believe all that is said about them.

There was a swamp and a creek flowing through the farm

and, from that large area, Ernie shot duck, geese, rabbits, 'roos and quail. His wife's quail dishes were renowned and it was said that people came for miles around to partake of them. Shortages occurred from time to time, however, and it was not always possible to harvest enough quail. That apparently did not bother Ernie unduly.

Down in the valley the big gums housed green parrots by the hundred and they were easy targets for a patient hunter. It took very little time to pick off a dozen or so for the pot and, when dressed out and cooked, it was easy to pass them off as the "real thing".

"Delicious quail," said one supposedly particular guest, tucking into a succulent parrot breast.

"Extraordinarily large, too," said the second.

And the story goes that Ernie gave all the credit to the very fertile land around the swamp! It made them grow big and fat, he told his guests.

It was at Jess's table that my wife and I first tasted kangaroo meat. She had put it to us all those years ago that the average Australian's snobbish attitude towards 'roo meat was born of ignorance. Anyone who tried it would be pleasantly surprised, she told us.

There was no hesitation on either of our parts. We wanted to try it. We did so and thoroughly enjoyed it. We have enjoyed it ever since and I have, in fact, on occasions, boned out the prime portions of a choice young buck, freezer-packed it and brought it home to England in my suitcase.

While we ate that first kangaroo meal and drank freely of the wine from the local vineyard, Ernie told of his wife's earlier deceptions. Both he and Jess were fond of curries and 'roo curry featured on their home menu many times. Unexpected guests/clients arrived one day and asked if they might have lunch after their ride. They were told that beef curry was on the menu and that they were welcome to indulge if they so desired. The meal was a great success.

Ernie explained to me that there was no intention of deceit involved. These folk had a long way to travel home. They had always enjoyed the Chitty hospitality. The food they had eaten was as good as any and better than most. Their mistaken attitude regarding the eating of 'roo meat would have deterred them from staying on for lunch and, since they were regarded as friends rather than clients, a little white lie was no big deal! That, Ernie insisted, was diplomacy rather than deceit. I agreed then and I do to this day.

Those same friends ate many more similar meals without knowing the meat source. In the circumstances ignorance was entirely blissful. My wife and I saw the point of Ernie's explanation and agreed that a completely opposite approach was our just entitlement. *We* would have been offended *NOT* to have known we were eating kangaroo. As we all agreed around that sumptuous table on many other occasions, it's "all in the mind".

Ernie left this world in November 1992 and the whole shire of Wanneroo mourned his passing. I know that I lost a very special friend with his passing and I know, too, that he is still sadly missed by many others who were privileged to hear his familiar greeting "G'day, Pal"!

I never met a better bushman. I never met a better horseman. And I certainly never knew a finer Aussie gentleman!

16
JACK

I have fished in many different places with many different people and, if you asked me to nominate one of my companions as "the best", I would be hard pressed. Somewhere very near to the top of the totem pole, however, would be one Jack Vasconcellos of Minnesota. He has the knack of being adaptable and the ability to catch fish in the worst possible conditions. I have always insisted that he can think like a fish and I'm sure that is so. But there is more to his ability than that. He handles tackle in a way that is especially appreciated by those who understand the finer points of what he is trying to achieve. Difficult to describe in words but devastating to the poor sucker who sits next to him fishless while he catches fish after fish! It has happened to me and I know!

Having said that, there *have* been times when I have held my own. In fact, I suppose, on balance we would cancel out in the worldwide scene. In the USA and on his "home ground", however, I have to struggle.

Jack Vas, as I call him, is not strictly a big fish man but he has caught his fair share of what the Americans refer to as "hunkers".

He lives on the banks of Big MacDonald Lake in Dent, Minnesota, where he hunts duck and grouse and catches fish to eat.

He is by far and away the best jig fisherman I have ever known and his assessment of weight to line strength, depth and temperature are away above my head. I *know* his think-ing. I understand it. But I cannot emulate it. He is too smart for me in the jig fishing field which, let's face it, *we* simply do not understand over here in the UK.

I was using jigs in this country for fourteen years before they suddenly became "dog nobblers"! I can claim without being too immodest that I was pretty damn good at it but I could not, can not, and never will be able to live up to the standards set by Jack Vas! Put us together and say – "OK, anything goes", and we would probably, over a week-long period, end up with about as many fish each. That is because I would revert to bait fishing and, in a bait situation, my expe-rience with various float tackles would give me an edge. In a jig-fishing situation, Jack would probably have two fish in the boat while I was fooling around putting bait on the hook!

The only time I can beat him is if we are both bait fishing with float tackle. Then I am the master. The trouble is, how-ever, that I left him a Hardy match rod several years ago and he has been practising! I can only hope that my old eyes are better than his when next we meet. We are within weeks of being the same age and we have the same love of the out-doors. We are not competitive – well, not until we get fishing together. Then it is a matter of honour.

It is a fact, of course, that we both cheat blatantly when we are fly casting, jigging or bait fishing for bluegills. Our limit is 30 fish per person – but our self-imposed limit is that they have to be *big* bluegills. Jack's idea of big changes every time I offer one for the keep net.

"Undersized," he snorts, and slips it back. So I cheat and up my score by one!

"I want you to be on top form," he said during one of my stays with him. "Tomorrow we have two guys from Illinois joining us and we have to have a fish fry. *We* are going to show these guys a thing or two about bluegill fishin'."

"What are the restrictions?" I asked.

"None at all," he replied. "Break out your floats and long bait rod!"

He and I shared a boat. His other guests shared another.

We all fished the same area which, in fairness to Jack, was one that he alone had located through sheer experience.

It was a hilarious occasion! Jack and I were in a highly competitive mood and it was a bait situation on a very hot afternoon.

I am not prepared to say which of us caught the more fish, or who claimed the biggest of the bunch, but we went ashore with a load of fish that kept Jack and his fillet knife busy for a long time. Jack and I talked of it often.

"How have you done?" asked the wife of one of the other pair.

"We done real good, honey," was the reply, and the fish were duly displayed. The lovely lady concerned looked him in the eyes and said, "Fine. But how many of those did *you* catch?"

It was all a lot of fun. It didn't matter a scrap but it was great for this old Limey to share the glory with the master in a situation where honour was at stake.

I know the vagaries of fishing all too well. I know how easy it is for two anglers to fish together in the same boat and for one to catch and the other to fail. My late brother Ken and I once fished with our tench floats almost touching each other. Our tackles and baits were absolutely identical and yet our score (if that is the correct word) in one short evening was 21 to nil. Whichever way you look at it, only sheer luck is involved in such a situation.

I once fished for crappie under Jack's guidance using identical rigs, jigs and tackle. Jack caught fish after fish; almost one per cast. I caught the odd one from time to time but, for the most part, I failed. And I became angry. I was *not* angry with Jack for beating me. I expected that. I was, however, angry with myself for not being able, at least, to contribute.

Jack had rigged us both with the right tackle. He had handled the boat, located the fish and described the procedure. The least I could do was pay him the compliment of catching a few fish. But I was hardly in the running and the harder I fished, the fewer fish came my way. In retrospect and after lots of discussion, I *know* exactly what I had done wrong.

I knew the fish were suspended at 13 feet and that they were vulnerable. I knew also that Jack was counting up to nine after he had cast his jig before retrieving. To him it was a simple matter. Par for the course, if you like. What I had failed to do was make my own rate of countdown identical to his. No two people count at the same speed. He had said he was counting to nine and he was making contact at each cast. I was counting to nine and either going over the top or too deep to score. What I should have done, and was probably too proud to consider, was ask Jack to count down *OUT LOUD* and confirm the timing on the second hand of my watch. By the time I had figured it out, the party was over and the fish had departed or gone off feed. It was, however, a lesson well learned and has since proved effective in the trout-fishing field.

Jack came to England for a month in 1984 (I have just phoned him to check and I cannot believe that over sixteen years have passed!). He and I left our respective ladies to themselves and spent the greater part of our time fishing. The timing of his visit was such that we caught the end of the summer trout fishing, the start of our recognised UK pike season and some of our better coarse fishing.

It is never easy to show a good friend a good time! I know there is not a single reader who will disagree with me regarding the "laying on" of fishing for someone special. I have tried it many times. I have succeeded beyond my wildest dreams on occasions, but for the most part things have not gone according to plan.

Willow Pool trout fishery, under the control of fisheries expert John Kalicki at the time, was one place where I could almost guarantee to catch a biggish trout to order. I had done so many times. I had not broken any records but I could claim a fair number of good fish up to 8lb. It was a super fishery but, alas, on the day we visited the water it was in dour and unproductive mood. I am prepared to admit that we were not up to the challenge but that does not alter the result.

I took Jack to a favourite lake to fish for pike. I had high hopes and since Jack regards a 10-pounder as a "trophy", I intended to show him some sport. Again, alas, the water was murky and the fish were not moving.

Jack was old enough, wise enough and gentleman enough to shrug his shoulders and agree that fishing was ever that way. I was disappointed, however, and I sensed that Jack was too.

Knowing that he was an expert with lures, jigs and other artificial baits, I took him to a prolific water where I had often enjoyed modest sport with plugs and spoons. We fished together in super surroundings, caught a few small pike and generally enjoyed a pleasant day together.

I had wanted Jack to catch a big pike. They were there to be caught, I knew. That Jack could handle a 20-pounder was never in doubt and I knew also that he had the skill to hook one. All he needed was a hint of luck and unfortunately it never came his way. Murphy's Law sent a 26-pounder to my rod and Jack had the dubious pleasure of putting the net under it. I said at the time that Murphy could have had my rod, reel and tackle box for Jack to have enjoyed that pleasure. Even so, it was my third largest pike ever and it helped me achieve a little of my own back.

"Some of us have got it; some of us ain't!" I told Jack's lovely wife, Dorothy, as we discussed the incident afterwards! Dorothy, however, was not impressed! She knew I had enjoyed too many fish meals in her home in Minnesota to be serious.

Jack and I, one year, fished every day for two weeks through 40 inches of ice! That, I have to add, tends to sort out the men from the boys! I could never hope to live with Jack in terms of ice fishing. It is a technique that needs skill, practice and experience. He had, and still has, all three.

Sometimes we fished outside; sometimes in the shelter of his little insulated fish house situated on the ice in front of his home. The walk to it was only a matter of a few hundred yards but we had to travel always on snow shoes. To me it was an adventure. Jack saw it as an everyday occurrence.

If we fished "indoors", we would put a couple of sticks of kindling in his little wood-burning stove and be stripped

125

down to shirt sleeve attire in about half a minute. When we fished outside, we would move from spot to spot (in that vast, white expanse of snow, everywhere looked the same to me!) and Jack would fire up the little motorised auger that churned its way through the ice in a matter of seconds. Then with tiny, two-foot wands, we would bait jighooks with wax-worm grubs and catch perch, bluegill, crappie and tulibee. Tulibee are members of the herring family and complete their spawning run under the ice.

Those were experiences I will never forget. I could tell a million stories of Jack Vas. They would all have to do with his sheer ability and adaptability.

He had no love for carp when I first met him but I pressed him to find us a venue. He took me to the Red River which forms the boundary between Minnesota and North Dakota.

Carp, I could see, were feeding everywhere and just for once in my life I was able to impress him. Jack was not aware that those great sheets of bubbles were caused by feeding carp but I proved it very quickly by catching one on a grain of sweet corn.

Within minutes he was fishing a few yards downstream of me and matching me fish for fish. We caught a dozen or so prime, common carp up to about 14lb. It was a horrendously snaggy situation and I can only say that I was full of praise for his handling skill.

Some anglers seem to be able to anticipate a carp's next move and counter it at once. Richard Walker could. Peter Thomas almost certainly still can. Jack learned the art very quickly. To the best of my knowledge he had never before been obliged to wrestle big fish out of such thick cover but he was very quickly master of the situation.

Just as he was when we fished fly together for trout on the overgrown and very weedy Test carrier stream in Hampshire. He needed showing just one time. From then on I knew I would be hard pressed to beat him. In fact I struggled to make it a tie!

I have said many times that there is a lot more to fishing than catching fish. That is not true as far as Jack Vas is concerned. He goes fishing to catch fish. The real joy of his fishing life is the battle between him and his chosen quarry. It is a battle he is never prepared to lose and, in truth, he hardly ever does!

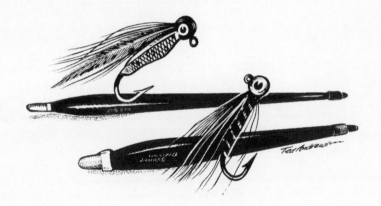

"Contrary Mary"

"I'd like you guys to try some of our moose steaks," said Mary up at Fort Chippewey in Northern Alberta. We had travelled the 200-mile-long ice road (there is no road except in winter!) and had met her and her husband Charlie purely by chance in that very, very cold environment. Mary and Charlie were Chippewean Indians (I object to calling them so since they are NOT Indians but Native Americans. However, as they refer to themselves that way, it is obvious they do not object.)

Just for the devil of it, as we all accepted the offer, I suggested they would be better remembered if cooked over a campfire in the snow. I was joking but Mary took me seriously. "No problem," she said. "We do it all the time." And she rustled up the meat and the big iron skillet.

Charlie had a fire going in about ten seconds flat. Mary began trimming slivers of fat off the huge steaks and here is where I let the side down, or so it seemed!

"What about the onions?" I asked.

Mary's look was colder than the surrounding snow.

"You DO NOT need onions with moose steaks!" she counselled. "You need only a little moose lard (from the rendered fat slivers) and salt."

Who was I to argue?

Soon the steaks were sizzling and we sat on straw bales to feast upon them in due course. Wonderful!

I have eaten, in my lifetime, some thirteen different forms of venison in various parts of the world but none was better than those moose steaks! With crisp new bread and nothing else other than black coffee from a beat-up billy-can, it was a meal, and an occasion, to be remembered.

As I wiped out the pan with the remaining crust, I thought, perhaps, that Mary was right. A sackful of onions could not have improved that repast and I shall not forget in future. On the other hand, of course, I may be sacrilegious when I know I am safe from Mary's fierce gaze!

17
TED

It has been my privilege over the years to meet a great many anglers from the American continent and to spend weeks on end in the desert, wilderness and mountains of that great part of the world. I have sweltered in the heat of Oregon. I have struggled with a backpack up the Rockies of Wyoming, and I have been eaten alive by horrendous mosquitoes in Montana. I have enjoyed the utter isolation of such areas but I confess that, although I have spent days and nights there alone, I have never been happier than when in the company of the late, great Ted Trueblood of Idaho.

Here was a true backwoodsman. A man who loved and respected the desolate places of his native land and who fought all his life to preserve them.

I met him in Missouri with another knowledgeable character, one Bill Hughes of Arkansas (who deserves a book in his own right but who is the subject of another chapter). They were so very different and yet they had so much in common. Ted was a laid-back, relaxed, quiet person; Bill was a salesman and a self-confessed bull-slinger. Both were fly-casting perfectionists. Both had been country bred. Both were total conservationists in the true sense of the word. They conserved but did not preserve because they knew that the one was wise while the other was foolish.

That week in Missouri was the only time I had the good fortune to be with them both together. Ted died in 1982, fifteen years after that first meeting. Journalists and outdoorsmen throughout the whole of the United States mourned his passing. Meeting him was a privilege; being accepted by him as a friend was an honour for me, since he did not suffer fools gladly. He had sympathy for those confined to towns and factories but he could not stand phonies. His one dread, he told me, was having to meet a "city guy dressed in a city suit" prior to one of his well-planned fishing trips. If you went fishing with Ted you ventured far into the outback or wilderness and you rolled out a sleeping bag at the end of the day.

In the morning you scraped off the frost, lit the campfire, put on the coffee pot and went to catch breakfast in the stream. When you returned it was highly likely that Ted would have the fire well livened up, bacon in the big frying pan sizzling alongside the trout he had already caught, and a second pan waiting for your contribution. The air would be filled with the aroma of coffee and pinewood smoke, and you would dry off your cold feet by the luxury of those burning logs in anticipation of breakfast and the day yet to come. And the next day and the next ... You never went for a day's fishing with Ted. You went for several days, a week or even more. You travelled through mountain passes and across deserts going from waterhole to waterhole. You gathered watercress and wild asparagus for camp meals at night, and you fished for a few hours each evening, and again each morning, before moving on elsewhere. At night you sat around the campfire drinking good bourbon whisky, and you filleted fish ready for the next day's meal. You dug holes to bury your trash, and you kept an eye open for bears. If, by chance, you were to spend two nights in the same camp while you exploited the fishing by day, you prepared a "Mulligan" or a pot roast immediately after breakfast. You brought the Mulligan (beef stew or whatever) to the boil on the campfire in the big iron Dutch oven. You transferred some of the campfire to a hole dug in the sand, placed the pot on top of the hot coals, shovelled the rest of the fire on top of the lid, covered the lot with sand or dirt, and went fishing. Eight hours later you returned and dug out that big iron pot to relish a savoury pot roast of beef, or a dish of stew too succulent for mere mortals to describe! And all the time the emphasis was on fishing and the catching of fish. Without fish, the rations in the ice box would quickly disappear and it was cheating to dig too deeply into reserves!

I recall days when we travelled many miles to fish for an hour or so in different streams and mountain lakes. I remember that Ted insisted I watched Old Faithful, the Yellowstone Park geyser, erupt when all I wanted to do was go fishing. I was far from happy that he wanted me to see the hot springs and other magnificent sights in that unique part of America, but how glad I am now that he made me do so without ever taking away the pleasures of catching all kinds of fish.

I remember my aching bones protesting in the heat of the day while his old four-wheel-drive truck chugged away across rocks and streams, sand dunes and wash-outs until we stopped for lunch. Cans of frozen beer were then rested on the hood to thaw out slowly while we hacked away at bread and mature cheese. Sheer bliss! All the time Ted would tell of the history of the area and explain the significance of certain features. Here there had been an earthquake; there were the "craters of the moon". When the temperature was 100°F plus, he took me down a cave or pothole where the ice lay several feet thick. An old Indian refrigerator, he called it. He was a mine of information.

I remember one night when we sat around a campfire after two days of travelling over rough country. I had no idea where we were but I had every confidence in my "guide". In the event of a breakdown, I knew we were unlikely ever to be in serious trouble, despite having not seen a living soul for over 36 hours. We had water to hand and there were fish for the catching. It would not be a luxurious existence but I knew we would not go hungry, nor would we die of thirst. We were due back within a week and our route was known to other people who would set out to find us if we failed to return. Ted loved the outdoors more than any man I ever knew, but he wisely took no chances.

As we talked on into the night, I mentioned my fear of getting lost and insisted that he tell me what to do in the event of – say – an accident which left me in charge. I was hesitant to ask at first but, despite having tried to figure out where we were, I was, to all intents and purposes, "bushed". That is to say, lost in desolate country.

Ted drew on his blackened pipe and told me I was the first companion he had ever known to take the trouble to ask. He could easily have a heart attack, he said (he had already recovered from one in 1968), and I was wise to take precautions. In the sand he drew rough maps, explained where we were and told me how to travel in relationship to the sun by day and the stars by night. Fortunately I was not called upon to do so. Nevertheless, the knowledge was a comfort to me despite my total lack of confidence. I understood Ted when he referred to that knowledge as "insurance". Getting lost, he told me, could be a terrifying experience but it ought not to be so.

The greatest enemy was panic, he said, and the first thing to do was to whip it. Sit down. Smoke a pipe, chew a piece of gum or eat a candy bar, or whatever else was available. Convince yourself that being lost does not mean you are in serious trouble. Look around you and bear in mind that you are alive and well. You need two vital things. Dry wood and water. You can live several days without food but you will die without water. Ted carried essential fire-lighting gear as a matter of course. He assumed, perhaps, that everyone else was as wise as he which, in my case and at that time, was not strictly true! He went on to explain how to survive the night (if necessary) by building some kind of shelter after lighting a fire to warm the ground upon which it was necessary to sleep. So simple and yet so wise.

Since those days, I have always carried a small bag of survival equipment. It holds two disposable lighters (I might lose one), a very sharp penknife, a stub of candle with three Vesta matches embedded in the wax, a magnifying glass, a small compass, a sacking needle and a length of waxed twine, two nails, a big safety pin, half a dozen aspirins, a small roll of

adhesive tape and a miniature bottle of Scotch. The latter is for morale more than medical purposes and the seal has not been broken for about fourteen years!

I learned a lot about survival from Ted but long before I met him I had learned the wisdom of carrying fire-lighting equipment. I will remember, for as long as I live, the sight of a packet of bacon rashers and a box of wet matches after a wet and windy night. I never cease to smile when I hear about, or see advertised, some of the weird and wonderful "survival" fire-making kits. I see no need for, or advantage in, flint strikers and weird blocks of magnesium that have to be shaved into shreds to start a fire. I have a survival book which tells me how to prepare tinder from a burned handkerchief and which will supply future fire-lighting needs until Judgement Day. The trouble is, it does not tell me how to light the handkerchief in the first place!

And I have asked myself a hundred times why I should

carry a tin box of tinder, a piece of flint and a steel striker when I can easily carry a few matches in a candle stub, a magnifying glass and a disposable lighter! My whole pack, including both lighters, takes up less room than any of the other "essentials" I have seen.

Paranoid about fire-lighting equipment I may well be. Cold, wet or hungry in the wilderness I certainly am NOT.

I hope never to be "bushed" again, for it brings, as I well know, a surge of sheer panic. I was once totally bushed in Australia and, despite knowing that I had friends within a mile or so, I felt that awful feeling in my gut that set me off in the wrong direction and would have had me going round in circles had I not steadied myself and remembered Ted Trueblood's advice. As it happened, I "reasoned" my way back to the edge of the dense bushland, saw what appeared to be a water dam half a mile away and headed for it. Before doing so I fired three shots into the air and waited. My thinking was simple. The temperature was in the 100°s Fahrenheit. I could make the dam easily enough and, if necessary, survive the night. The universal three-shot distress signal would reach my friends and let them know of my problem. They would know of the dam's existence and I would see them heading towards it when they came for me.

I suffered some indignity as a result of being lost but I received the compliments of two first-class bushmen for the course I had followed. I readily accepted, however, that this had been due to Ted Trueblood's steadying influence all those years previously. I can think of no-one who has impressed me more by simple logic allied to a colourful imagination. The conversations we held as we sat around our many campfires were the very stuff of survival and the love of wild places. He made me think of what I would do in the event of a serious problem. He added a lot to my earlier desert training, and I like to think he talked because he knew I would listen and benefit from his words. He was not by nature an extrovert and even today I accept that he paid me the ultimate in compliments.

"You're not such a greenhorn as you pretend to be," he

said once. "You know how we got here by way of the water holes. If need be you could get back the same way because you've taken note."

I could not have claimed such confidence but I was gratified that Ted had noticed my attempts at simple observation.

We were together in a big, wide and somewhat hostile world. It was a real world but Ted, quite deliberately, and with mischief in his soul, would turn it into one of fantasy.

He would sip on an enamel cup of bourbon and suddenly toss a question my way.

"What would you do if ...?" he would ask, posing some improbable situation. I would think for a few moments and then answer to the best of my ability. Ted would grin with delight if I gave the right reply but he would snort in disgust if I missed the obvious point of his question.

Today, many years after those lessons, I find myself studying where I have been as seriously as the trail ahead. It is a fact that a tree or feature viewed ahead looks entirely different when viewed from behind, and the secret of back tracking is to recognise what you have left behind! It is a simple strategy; one that is used by aboriginals all over the world and one which I now follow quite instinctively in unknown territory.

Out on the great Owyhee lake, where the mountains meet the desert in Oregon, Ted showed me how to fish for largemouth bass with plastic worms. It is a simple enough procedure but based on a knowledge of depth and temperature.

Find a spot where the bottom temperature coincides with the bass's preferred feeding temperature and you are in business. I caught my first and only 6-pounder in his company and on his instructions. He was even more delighted than I was. We tried to return it but it had been hauled up from the depths and because of its obvious distress we dispatched it. Cooked over the campfire coals it served for two hearty meals and I have seldom tasted better.

That same night we talked into the dark hours while our rods, resting against convenient boulders, fished for breakfast by themselves. Every so often one would jump and another channel catfish or bullhead would end up in the cooler box. Those cool desert nights were indeed very special. So, too, were the days and nights spent on the Snake River in Idaho. Carp, catfish, bass and trout came our way as we floated that super river day after day, and I remember our many bank sessions after dark seeking whatever came our way. Catfish were our main quarry but carp did not know they were not supposed to take fish portions and, every so often, an expected big catfish would turn out to be a wild common carp.

On one particular float trip, Ted, having seen carp working the scum lanes and feeding on the surface, decided to try to catch carp on fly tackle. If we did things right, he said, it would be possible, and we set forth full of hope.

We failed as it happened, but, in the process, we caught a long stringer of other fish. At the end of our float, Ted pulled the boat into shore and began filleting our catch. I, meanwhile, saw a small slack which I thought might be interesting to fish from the bank.

A tin of sweet corn, a light outfit and a No. 10 hook were all I needed. Never did bites come so quickly. Never did common carp fight so hard. Never did I whoop and shout so much or so loudly as I did with each contact.

I missed strikes. I lost fish. I suffered the shakes in my anxiety to recast, and still I caught, I believe, 24 common carp in about $1\frac{1}{2}$ hours. The exact figure remains vague in memory but I know there were over twenty and I *know* that I had never caught so many carp in so short a session ever before.

Plans to go back again have been frustrated but I am sure those carp will still be there. They are unsophisticated fish since no one rates them in the USA. They will not be deterred by cold nights or drops in water temperature, nor will they be at all finicky about picking up baits. Those I caught, using the simple, hand-held, touch-leger style almost tore the rod from my hands!

I never caught a really big fish from the Snake. But I know a man who did!

Years ago, before the installation of hydroelectric dams, sturgeon ran the Snake River. There are many kinds of sturgeon, of course, and I don't know the Snake's particular species. I do know, however, that catching one was a very specialised business and that Ted Trueblood set out at one stage to do so.

I have no idea of the method he used or the bait involved, but what I can tell you is that the fish Ted caught was in excess of 100lb. I recall, too, his remarks after he had caught it: they were to the effect that he didn't have to bother about big fish any more.

If anyone asked him, he would simply say he had already caught one!

A nice touch that but typical of the man's dry sense of humour.

Once, as we crossed the great plains of the Idaho wilderness (or was it Montana or Oregon?), he pointed out a particularly barren area stretching to the far horizon.

"Yonder," he said, "is known as 'No Cabbage Flat'."

When I asked the reason for its odd name, he put on a puzzled expression.

"Do you see any cabbages?" he asked.

He had invented names for many of the spots he knew well and, over the years, his close friends knew where he meant when he mentioned "Fluster Flat". There had been so many gamebirds there on one occasion, he told me, that he had become flustered for the first and only time he could recall. Even his dog had gone off at half cock and he had been obliged to call a halt and settle them both before proceeding. Hence Fluster Flat.

Illegal Bay he had so named because he had encountered a very sick bald eagle there on one of his hunting trips!

Somewhere high up in the Rocky Mountains, Ted taught me how to make a bough bed – or at least his own particular version of one. I had loaned my air mattress to the third member of our party – one Charlie Bowen – who insisted on sleeping above ground in the camper truck. I knew it was possible to make a soft bed from spruce boughs, having read about it previously, but I had never made one before.

"It's not a correct description," said Ted. "It's a twig bed

139

really. It's made up from the feathery tips of the boughs and not the boughs themselves."

Ted regarded a small axe as one of his most important accessories. His own weighed $1^3/_4$lb and he truly believed that it was the piece of equipment most likely to save his life. I have always been happy with the heavy-duty bowie knife which hangs on my belt unnoticed until I need it. With it I can dress game or fish, cut down saplings for shelter, and chop up kindling for the essential fire. It is razor sharp, made of good Sheffield steel and, on this occasion, I used it to make my bed. It took a long time. In a slight hollow, I piled up an incredible heap of springy twigs, tossed a blanket over it and, when darkness fell, I retired to the pine-scented luxury of the best outdoor bed I have ever known. My sleep was dreamless and the sounds of the night served as my lullaby. My only regret was that I could not take it with me when we moved on the next day.

I made bough beds often after that but none ever seemed as splendid as my first. Without Ted's advice I might well have spent many uncomfortable nights out in the mountains but Ted Trueblood was always helpful to those less fortunate.

He was the greatest outdoor writer I have ever been privileged to meet, and also the greatest conservationist. He could beat me at fly-casting and he was a boat-handler of great skill. I could perhaps hold my own with him when it came to a free-for-all aimed at putting fish on the table, but it was not of our nature to be competitive. We were two of a kind in that our hearts went out to those city-dwellers all over the world who did not have our kind of opportunity. We sought always to defend our right to fish and hunt and enjoy the great outdoors to the full. We were agreed on that but it was there that the differences tended to emerge.

I have always despised those who would take away my heritage. Ted always viewed them with sincere pity. That, no doubt, places him one notch on the totem pole higher than me but I do not mind. I have always felt privileged to have known him and I will always remember the reasoning he put before me after his heart attack in 1968.

"Don't wait too long," he counselled. "If you wait until tomorrow, tomorrow may never come."

His coronary came in February and, in his own words, scared the living daylights out of him. By July he was wading his treasured streams for trout. By October he was hunting chukars in the hills.

"Seize the day," said this wise and lovable outdoorsman.

"If you can't get something done that should be done – to hell with it. You couldn't do it if you were dead either!"

I doubt if I have followed his advice as well as I might have done, but I have always believed he was right. And bearing that in mind today more than ever before, I will drink to his memory in good bourbon whisky and recall his passion for the outdoors.

When the winter has passed and I sit beside my own campfire once more, I shall hope to enjoy again those special privileges which Ted Trueblood made me appreciate even more. To sit and watch the everlasting stars appear. To listen to the coyotes talking across the valley while the smoke rises and fills the darkening sky with the scents of the wild woods. And seize the day.

18
GOATHEAD

How Bill Hughes of Arkansas acquired the name "Goathead" had nothing to do with our friendship. It had come about during the picture promotion of a particular four-wheel-drive vehicle with "mountain goat qualities", and the name stuck. He was introduced to me as Goathead Hughes and I occasionally called him by that name during our travels together, but I have always known him as Bill Hughes – the Arkansas Hillbilly.

Perhaps my introduction will be better appreciated if I let him tell the story himself. He wrote it up in a book entitled *The Unedited Original Manuscript of my Life and Work*, which he completed in 1988. It is a fascinating volume and I am privileged to own one copy of a very limited edition.

Here is how Goathead described our first meeting. The details are embellished and some of the facts are not strictly true, but the overall picture is more or less accurate.

"I'm home from travelling the road selling Sporting Goods, especially, fishing tackle on Friday night in Jacksonville, Illinois and having slept late on Saturday morning I'm up, in the kitchen having a cup of coffee with my very dear wife, when the door bell rings and Martha goes and opens the door and comes back to tell me, 'There is someone out there trying to imitate a Southerner that wants to see you, Podner.' As I opened the door I saw a short man, big round belly, baldheaded, wearing a pair of seersucker pants that are 4 to

143

5 inches too big for him around the waist, rolled up about 4 inches at the bottom of each leg, an open necked tan sport shirt that is too large for his shoulders, also. I'm hesitating very cautiously as he greets me with that 'Podner' bull, looking him over trying to think who is trying to pull a joke on me. His old busted out cloth shoes told an old shoe 'dog' that they were not his nor his size. So, I just floated with the tide and said, 'What did you want?' (If I can get him to talk long enough I can figure out this ungodly, imitation hillbilly accent.) Finally, he couldn't take it any longer and 'gave his milk down' by converting to his normal English lingo and introduced himself, with a very friendly grin that said 'I'm your kind of folks' disarming me, completely, as he said, I'm Fred J. Taylor from London, England, visiting me old friend down the street apiece, Charley Bowen, who has told me so much about you that I wanted to meet you, especially since we are both engaged in the same business in two different countries.'

"So, I invited him in, cautiously, introduced him to Martha who poured him a cup of coffee and thus began one of the greatest genuine friendships two men ever had.

"I wish that I could write as well as he can and as interestingly as he, but I'm not an author, columnist, outdoor writer, master fisherman, raconteur, ferreter, rabbit and hare hunter, kangaroo hunter, wing shot; I'm just simply not a world traveller, not a member of the International Fisherman's Hall of Fame inducted into such with such a celebratory as General Mark Clark, nor am I one of the survivors of the 'Rats of Tobruk'. The two things that we have in common are that we are former poachers and are fishing tackle salesmen; he being the Sales Director of the F. Goddard Co., a London Fishing Tackle Company, and I am a Manufacturer's Sales Representative Company President."

Sometimes the old goathead can be embarrassing!

I never wore seersucker pants in my life, and I certainly never knocked on Bill's door! I was taken there and introduced to him correctly by my good friend Charles T. Bowen. I did, however, say "Howdy Podner" when we met.

144

Among all the embellishments, lies and half-truths there remains one indisputable fact. That meeting in 1967 was indeed the start of a genuine friendship that has lasted until his death. I tried very hard to visit him every time I went to the USA and before he retired I tried very hard to entice him over to England. He was, however, not a world traveller. His business kept him active in many different States and he thought nothing of hopping planes to and from various cities to sell his "lines". He was always a high-pressure salesman and he knew how to vary his approach to suit his client's needs. That, he said, was important!

His phone bill was horrendous. So much so that the tax authorities at one stage questioned its validity.

"Don't you talk about anything other than business on your telephone?" asked the inspector. "Surely you cannot claim all this is business!"

"Damn right it is," replied Bill. "When I ask a client how he's keeping, how his kids are doing at school, how his wife is bearing up after her operation and what the weather's like over there in Kentucky, I'm establishing a relationship that will, hopefully, end in a sale."

My own sales approach was similar in many respects but I could never resort to the "hard sell". Bill and I disagreed on that point but it never affected our friendship.

I have often tried to add up how many miles we travelled together in one or other of his big station wagons but we really took no account of distance. There was always an atmosphere of total relaxation when he was at the wheel. High pressure salesman he may well have been but all that vanished between calls. At around 4.00 p.m. each day, as he drove with one hand casually on the steering wheel, he would announce that it was "hog-rind time". This meant that we had to pull in somewhere, pick up a six-pack of beer and a couple of large bags of pork rinds. "Pork scratchings" I believe they are called in the UK, but I have never found a product anywhere else in the world to compare with those snacks he and I enjoyed daily on our travels. The beer was of a fairly low alcohol content and always ice-cold. It had to be. Otherwise it would be like all other American lager-type beers; totally undrinkable!

The American Fishing Tackle Manufacturers Association put on their Annual Exhibition in Chicago during my first stay in the USA, and I found myself being introduced to the media and a great many sales organisations. Bill continually introduced me as "The World's Greatest" this, that or other, much to my embarrassment. When I told him to ease up on that kind of stuff he grinned and said, "It's for me as well as you!"

Bill, it has to be said, indulged very occasionally in a "bender". Not often, but just to celebrate the odd occasion. One of his partners had decided to break away from the organisation and the final details were settled at that particular exhibition. Those details are unimportant. What mattered at the time was that Bill and Vaughn (the third partner) were now in complete control. The name of the Company was changed and Bill announced that he was "gonna tie one on". In his parlance that meant he was going to get good and drunk!

Vaughn and I shared a hotel room with him and we retired to it early. Not necessarily to sleep but to sip a little sour-mash bourbon and await his return. In the early hours of the morning he could be heard leaving the elevator outside our room.

"Quick," said Vaughn. "Pretend to be asleep or he'll bend our ears all night."

I pulled the sheet over my head. Vaughn snored very gently.

Bill crashed through the door, looked around him, tottered unsteadily to the bed and shouted, "Well, kiss my ass."

At that, he collapsed on the bed and passed into oblivion. He was still fully dressed, even to his collar and tie, when we woke him for stand duty after daybreak!

I had dressed casually for the whole of that five-day show simply because I was not on duty. I had no need for jacket, collar and tie when all I had to do was keep my eyes open for possible "stories". When the rest of the "gang" came off duty they immediately put on open-necked short-sleeved shirts and went out to the nearest restaurant or bar. I joined them at their invitation every night but failed to notice on the last occasion that they were all "properly dressed". No-one had told me we were going to the so-called Millionaires Club for dinner!

The doorman politely refused me entry while Bill and Vaughn arranged for a table for eight people.

I was not in the least unhappy about not being allowed to enter. I knew the form and accepted the situation.

"We will rent you a jacket, sir," said the doorman. I declined.

"Cancel the table," said Bill and Vaughn together. "If our English buddy ain't good enough we'll eat somewhere else."

"We'll lend you a jacket and tie free, sir," said the doorman. I declined again and said with a grin, "You never know *where* it's been!"

There was a little more discussion as I tried to explain that I was very happy to go back to the hotel and leave them to enjoy themselves. I was *not* in any way offended but it seemed my colleagues were! They took my arm and walked me down the block.

Among Bill's staff was one Sam Appleby, known affectionately as Big Sam. He weighed 300lb and was about 6′4″ tall!

"Hey, Sam," said Bill. "Lend this goddam Limey your coat and tie." Sam handed both items over and I put them on at once. I saw what was going through his mind and went along with him.

We retraced our steps to the Club to be met by the same doorman. Sam's jacket hung around me like a sack. It was a huge double-breasted affair and the sleeves were at least six inches too long but, along with Sam's tie, it qualified me for entry. Willie and I made believe we were intending to change our minds and dine.

"Jacket and tie as per instructions," I explained. "That's what you demanded; that's what you've got."

The doorman protested but I insisted that I should be allowed entry.

Bill threw down the challenge.

"Tell me where this guy's breaking the rules," he demanded. "Is he wearing a jacket and tie, or not?"

The doorman almost exploded. I could see the frustration on his face and he was obviously uncertain what action to take.

At last I could stand it no longer. I laughed out loud and let him see he was the victim of a hoax. The relief on his face was a joy to behold and he joined us in the general laughter.

Chicago has remained one of my best-loved cities and I recall the incident with affection every time I visit.

Illinois was the hub of Bill's business venture but it was not his favourite State. He was an "Arkansas Hillbilly" (or so he claimed) and was never happier than when on his home territory. Eventually he moved back to Rogers, Arkansas, and ran his operation from there. He introduced me to moonshine, smoked carp, beans and cornbread, and Beaver Lake. He introduced me to the wonderful folks of Arkansas and I will never forget their genuine hospitality.

The nearest airport to Rogers was at Fayetteville and he and I planned, one holiday weekend, to fly there from Springfield, Illinois via St. Louis. Since I booked all my flights in the UK before leaving, Bill insisted that I be sure to book the leg from St. Louis to Fayetteville well in advance. The schools would be breaking up and seats on planes would be as rare as feathers on a frog, he insisted. I booked my flights early. Bill confirmed them on the day before travel and we arrived at St. Louis in good time. At the gate there was no rush for seats. In fact we two appeared to be the only passengers present. Had we made a mistake regarding times? Not according to the flight information shown above the desk.

It turned out that we had the complete plane and the services of the charming hostess to ourselves!

"A drink, gentlemen?" she asked immediately after take-off.

We decided that a couple of dry Martinis would help see us through the trip and went through the motions of paying for them.

"It's hardly worth opening the cash box since you're the only two passengers on board. Have these on the house," said the young lady with a smile. And, as she was likely to be bored with the flight anyway, did we mind if she joined us? Of course we did not.

I don't know who told the more lies or drank the more Martinis during that flight but since the hostess insisted that we "have another drink, gentlemen" every few minutes, it didn't really matter. Both Bill and I were well past caring when we arrived at our destination. So much for the over-crowded holiday rush.

I loved Beaver Lake and enjoyed some wonderful fishing there. I also made a carp fisher out of Bill who, until then, had no real interest in catching them. Not for him the chucking out of a bait to await the fish's pleasure. He *hunted* his fish, as did all his colleagues, by casting lures (or plugs or spoons, plastic worms or "baits" that were not strictly baits as we know them) and searching for them wherever they happened to be lying.

Fishing in many parts of the USA more or less revolves around the pursuit of bass, and bass have to be hunted. You do not lie in wait for bass; the bass lie in wait for you. Or whatever you have on offer! So when I decided that I would have a go at catching a carp back in 1972, Bill shrugged his shoulders and informed me he was going to the liquor store to pick up a couple of cases of beer. Perhaps I should let him tell the story from here.

"Taylor put his open-faced spinning reel and 6lb test line on to one of my 9'0" soft-actioned, Steelhead River Rods. Gene Thresher said he would never handle a carp on that kind of tackle and Taylor grinned, tying on a No. 6 trout hook. Thresher told him that hook would never hold a Beaver Lake carp – these carp were much too big for such tackle.

"Taylor peeled off the rind of a sliced loaf and pinched most of what was left on to the hook. He did not ball it up but left it loose and fluffy and referred to it as "flake". He pinched a split shot six inches above the hook, cast out about 50–60 feet and let the bread sink slowly into 30 feet of water. He laid the rod butt on a chair with the tip over the boat rail and went to get another chair to sit on. As I started to leave to get the beer, the rod jumped and banged the rail. We both ran for it but the line was slack. The fish had either broken the line or straightened the hook, I thought, but, as he reeled in, neither had happened. Only the bread was missing.

"He re-baited and cast again to the same spot and, in less than five minutes, had the damnedest show going that the guys at the Marina had ever seen. The carp stayed close to the bottom but Brother Taylor proceeded to put on an exhibition of how to handle a big fish on light gear."

There is a lot more, and Bill is generous with his praise for what was nothing more than an average piece of tackle control.

The fish weighed 15lb and was duly landed (or boated) after someone dug out a salmon-sized "dip-net" from the nearby store.

That part of the tale is of no greater importance but Bill's next remark, in my opinion, was!

"Taylor immediately made a carp fisherman out of me! As I had another of these River Rods, I rigged up the other one in a hurry and got Fred to show me how to install the flake.

I completely forgot to go for the beer!"

Bill and I, according to his report, took nineteen carp (all in double figures) by 4.30 that afternoon. I am quite sure we caught that number – but I think, perhaps, Bill included the few we caught at dawn the next day. Not that it matters. We had ourselves a great time and I was totally stricken by the pristine quality of those big, wild, torpedo-like common carp. I was also impressed by the fact that although the boat dock was covered in frost at dawn, Bill and I were sunbathing in the afternoon.

"You don't like the weather in Arkansas? Stick around for ten minutes!" That is Bill's apt description of what that lovely State is all about, and there are a few English carp anglers still around who can vouch for the truth of it.

Bill and I often discussed the trip which I organised some time later when a dozen English carp anglers went out at a

151

bad time of year for carp fishing, but who enjoyed American hospitality at its very best.

Bill and his lovely wife, Martha, arranged a smoked fish supper for us, the media, several outdoor writers, game wardens and local guides, soon after the English contingent arrived. On the menu were Coho Salmon, Steelhead, Lake Trout and Arctic Char. All had been processed in Bill's electrically controlled smoker. All were eaten and enjoyed.

Only when the Fish and Game Warden Supervisor asked Bill if he had used a dough ball for the char, was the secret unveiled. The Arctic char was, in fact, a Beaver Lake carp. That is how Bill tells the story and it is true enough but he *had* also informed me and I was in on the secret.

I recall those days every time I write to Bill in his retirement and I know full well that I miss the old Goathead more today than ever before.

The English anglers' fondness for carp *and* their reluctance to put them on stringers for eating later, gave our hosts cause to smile tolerantly but I know full well that we sowed good seeds when we were present at Beaver Lake. I know that, today, although some carp are retained to be eaten, those caught and not kept for food are released at once to the deep waters of Beaver Lake.

Time passes, of course, and memories fade, but the value of stories told does not normally decrease with age. Each time I read them I tell myself that another bullshine session with that cotton-pickin' Hillbilly no-hoper is long overdue! God willing, I'll rectify it soon enough.

Footnote: Alas, Bill died at the age of 84 in Rogers, Arkansas in March after a long illness.

19
"CATFISH CARL"

I could write a book about Carl Loutit but I have no serious space left. He is a native from Manitoba and has an Indian ancestry. How I *hate* that word "Indian" when applied to Natives of the American Continent! These wonderful conservationists are *NOT* Indian! They are American! They have rights and, of course, they have problems, but the facts are that these so-called "Red Indians" have, over many years, been suppressed by the laws of the white man, who has always deemed himself to be superior. My immediate reaction is to snort in disbelief, "Superior my foot".

I taught Carl how to make a "Fish Mornay" in his own kitchen in Lockport, Manitoba. I also taught him how to fry fish portions in a superior batter. All it was, was a simple frying batter but, with the accompaniment of a couple of fresh eggs! No big deal! But Carl has done a thousand fish fries for his clients since.

Carl is a Red River guide and a good one at that. So good, in fact, that he is known as "Catfish Carl".

He is also known as "Shanks" since he lost his driving licence for five years and has not bothered to renew it!

With others, we have shared the "Cold Camp" in the Winnipeg River wilderness area we call Jackfish Bay. Our campfires have been very special and many a deer-hunting party has caught the smell of the wood smoke and homed in to share our cuisine. Carl loves to cook and he is never too proud to learn.

I could tell a million tales of Carl but I'll settle for the knowledge that he has become a true friend over the years. He is a brilliant, self-taught guitarist and among my many pleasures are memories of "picking along" with Carl around a campfire under the frost-spangled pines.

We play, we sing, we imbibe a little red wine or rye whisky and we promise always *not to* "*hurt* ourselves" by over-indulging! It does not always happen that way, but whatever the outcome, our dream times, under the canvas of the big tent, are *never* troubled. In that particular piece of God's country we are always at peace!

20
NEWT

I first met Newt at Rogers, Arkansas, in 1973 when I took a group of English carp fishers over to Beaver Lake. It was April and spring was late. Snow still lay on the surrounding Ozark hills and the air was filled with more. An old friend, Bill Hughes, came with a group of friends to meet the plane at Joplin, Missouri and, after introductions and some late night socialising, a dozen weary anglers were bedded down for the night at Prairie Creek Motel on the banks of Beaver.

The sequence of events remains somewhat blurred but one of the first of many hospitable gestures made by those wonderful middle-west Americans came from Newt.

He ran a service station and a used-car emporium in Rogers, some 10 miles from the lake.

"You'll need wheels," he said. "Send someone over and I'll sort you out an automobile for your two-week stay. I'll take care of the tax and insurance but you'll have to buy your own gasoline."

We were duly presented with a big station wagon which became the lifeline of our stay. What it would have cost to hire such a vehicle is anyone's guess. It cost us the price of the petrol it used!

"You are all invited to the Cabin tonight," said Newt on the second day of our visit. "We're having beans 'n' cornbread so I hope you like it."

At first the Brits had some doubt as to the menu. Was this

155

man doing a Beverly Hill Billy wind up? Or was the meal to be a genuine beans 'n' cornbread supper? I had no doubts whatsoever. I had been before and I knew all about beans 'n' cornbread suppers in that cabin on the banks of the War Eagle River! I knew this would be a much more luxurious event than it had been made to appear and I knew also that the eyes of a dozen English anglers would be opened before the witching hour.

Beans! Several gallons of them in a big, black, iron pot had simmered all day long with massive chunks of ham cut from Arkansas hogs. Yellow corn bread, freshly baked and served hot with mountains of butter accompanied those deep plates of superb American fare. That in itself would have been enough but, of course, there was more food of many kinds on offer.

Cheese dips and pecan pies, banana cakes and orange jellies, fried chicken and smoked fish, bourbon whisky and ice-cold beer were followed by coffee made as only Americans know how. And throughout it all Newt kept up a non-stop patter which was designed quietly to discredit English anglers generally and to assess their reaction. It has to be said that his motives were quickly recognised and accepted in just the right spirit. Newt was of the opinion that a person who could not "take a bit of stick" was not worthy of attention. He learned quickly that we were all very much of a kind.

I have, over the years, used many of Newt's favourite expressions to make a point and I have yet to meet anyone with as many as he could call to mind.

Some are quite unrepeatable here but, in the main, they were fair comment in a particular situation. It was said that a certain famous American comedian came to fish with Newt for a whole week in order to pick up some of his remarkable sayings.

"Look at the Limey over there," he said, pointing to one of the group who was obviously enjoying the food. "He's eatin' like he's gonna get laid off, ain't he?"

Of the crappie down below the boat in 40 or more feet of water he would say, when they were biting, that they were "as thick as used-car dealers in hell". Anyone not too well-blessed with intelligence or common sense would be referred to as being "as thick as a truckload of toilet seats".

A person in a state of excitement would be "poppin' like a cat eatin' fat meat".

Anything or anyone considered to be on the warm side was said to be "as hot as a duck in a pepper patch".

I could fill a book with his sayings alone but there was more to him than a list of funny remarks.

Newt could also be a storyteller. He changed the locations around to suit the story occasionally and he often changed the story to suit a particular situation. None of which detracted from the story itself. He was an outdoorsman with a love of hunting in its truest sense, which means the pursuing of fish and game by all legitimate methods to provide food for the table. He was what the British field sportsman would refer to as a pot-hunter, and the following tale has to do with one of his pot-hunting ventures. It was told to me by Bill Hughes, his lifelong friend, who assures me it is true.

He and Newt set off one morning just before daylight to hunt geese on the first day of the season. Even at that early hour, however, all the "blinds" (hides) were occupied by other hunters and they were obliged to move on elsewhere. The pheasant season was open and, after due consultation, it was decided to drive several miles through corn country and try to flush a brace of pheasants from a favourite haunt. As they proceeded in the half-light, Newt called to Bill to halt.

"Stop the car, Willie," he ordered. "I gotta go."

Bill pulled in to the side but Newt was not happy with the choice of spot.

"Not here, Willie. Pull up further into the clearing. This ain't just a leak I need; it's a squattin' job!"

Bill did as requested and, as Newt walked off into the clearing, Bill handed him his 12-guage shotgun.

"Take it with you, Newt," he said. "You never know, you might kick up an old cock bird."

Newt took the gun, leaned it up against the tall yellow corn, dropped his pants and squatted.

A second or two later a great skein of geese flew low and slow over his head. Newt stood up, pointed his old piece at the passing birds, fired and shucked out three empty shells. Three geese folded up and fell. All were dead in the air before they hit the ground and, as Bill stood amazed and truly impressed with his expertise, Newt, with pants still around his ankles, squatted down again.

"Come pick 'em up, Willie," he ordered. "I ain't through yet!"

"April Fool"

Lofty was a poacher and the police and gamekeepers kept a wary eye open for him all year round. He poached for food, fished the local streams for eels, and snared rabbits for the table. He was, by strange coincidence, since he had never fished for salmon in his life, a fly-tier of some considerable skill. He collected feathers, fur, wool and other bits and bobs to keep him occupied during his off-season respite. Some of his classic salmon flies were a joy to behold.

Late, very late, on April 1st one year, Lofty was stopped by the local bobby and accused of poaching. Understandably so, because two pheasant tails were sticking out of his small haversack!

On inspection, however, the bag was seen to contain a dozen or so pheasant tail feathers set into two bottle corks. Lofty had been to visit a keeper friend who had saved him the feathers for his fly dressings. Despite his odd poaching forays, Lofty was never greedy and this particular keeper saw him as an ally in many respects. It was worth a pheasant now and then, he said, to know what was going on in and around the village. Lofty and he had a kind of understanding!

"April fool, officer," said Lofty when seen to be not guilty and, to be fair, the officer took it all in good part.

"There will be other nights," he said with a grin. And Lofty knew that would be so.

In the local, next day, Lofty recounted the adventure.

"I don't know about the midday ending," he said. "It was nearly April 2nd when he searched me but I reckon that still counted. And anyway," he went on,

159

"there are certain things a bloke just does not do. One of 'em is poach pheasants in April, and he should have known that!".

21
PETER

Peter Holbrook lives in an old farmhouse surrounded by timber country that is magnificent to behold. He farms an acreage that grudgingly provides his living, but he loves what he does. He points to the land around him and insists that he need never go hungry when there are wild pigs, goats, turkeys, rabbits and ducks as well as fish for the taking.

He milks a house cow, gathers free-range eggs, and produces his own beef, pork and mutton. He reaps annual harvests of opossum for their skins, and goats for their meat and wool. His lifestyle is extremely tough but in many respects I am envious.

I would not say that he was a big fish expert, or that he was particularly adept at using fishing tackle, but he does know a great deal about eels. New Zealand eels, that is. To look at them you would find it difficult to notice any difference between those and our own eels. They appear exactly the same but perhaps that is easily understood. To be able to spot the differences between species, you have to put the two together and examine them. What chance is there, I wonder, of comparing eels that live on opposite sides of the world and migrate at different times together?

The biggest eel Peter ever caught weighed 25lb but he assured me when we met that there were much bigger ones to be caught in the fantastic waterways of his beloved North

161

Island. He had heard tell of 50-pounders being caught on several occasions, he said.

I first went to New Zealand in 1981 and, by chance, spent some time in his area, known as Te Kuiti. I did not meet him then but he heard of my visit and wrote to me c/o one of the magazines on my return. He came originally from the English Midlands, he told me, and that if and when I came again I was to be sure and contact him. We exchanged a correspondence and two years later I met him in his local pub.

It was some time before I spotted the eel in a glass case above the bar and, when I did, I assumed it was one from the ocean. It weighed 22lb.

"No. No. It's a freshwater eel," said Peter. "Really it's nothing special!"

I was in New Zealand to fish for trout but I was already finding it hard to follow the tourist route. I like to do my own thing!

I am not an eel fanatic and I see no point in returning eels to the water, but I do enjoy eel fishing for fun. I fancied a dabble at those antipodean monsters and said so there and then.

A voice from a nearby table said, "I'll take you tomorrow morning if you want to go."

Peter could not join us on that venture and so I went with Vic (I think that was his name) and another Kiwi at dawn next day. I had been told not to worry about tackle but I was somewhat surprised to see none whatsoever on the old Land Rover.

After a horrendous journey over mountain passes and gorges, which took about an hour and a half to negotiate, and scared me half to death, we arrived at a small stream no more than 6 inches deep for the most part. Where, I wondered, could eels live here? And how on earth could we catch them?

My host tied big cod hooks to a couple of landing net handles to make mini-gaffs and walked into the stream. The technique was simple and hilariously effective. Here and there were deep holes and overhangs near the bank. A prod with the handle scared the eels out into the shallow stream where they tried to escape. The trick then was to "skin hook" them as they wallowed upstream and to keep only selected specimens for smoking later.

It may sound sadistic to eel lovers but in fact it is a very effective and humane exercise. The minor skin wound inflicted by the gaff does the creature much less harm than wrestling with it to remove a bait hook from its gullet. We returned those we caught, apart from one 7-pounder which was taken for the table. It was not the kind of fishing I had expected, but I could not deny that participating was sheer fun. I was glad then to have met Peter.

I only had fly rods with me when he took me bait fishing along the Mokau River. Here he told me he had caught large numbers of big eels and that long casts would not be necessary. A chunk of mutton, well past its sell-by date, was all we had for bait but it was good enough.

"Put any you catch in the sack and then fish close to the sack," Peter instructed. "The more disturbance they make the more others will be attracted."

I didn't believe it then, but I do now!

The first eel took some time to smell out the bait but it took immediately below the rod tip. It is not easy trying to handle a big eel on a fly rod, line and leader, and it goes without saying that I lost the bigger specimens. I could only manage the "small ones" up to about 6lb on my stripped wet fly hooks, but the more eels I put in the sack the more bites I experienced.

On my third visit to his lovely country, I was able to spend more time with him and I went prepared with tackle suitable for eels. Fairly hefty ledger rods and lines, and heavy lines.

"First we will go on a turkey hunt," said Peter. "After that we will have a hangi and the next day we will go eeling."

When you can point a .22 rifle as straight as Peter, coming home with a brace of turkey is not difficult. Hitting a flying target at 100 yards, however, is not as easy as he made it appear. I swear I have never seen better shooting anywhere.

We hung the brace of birds and plucked them later, saving

the livers and necks for eel baits. Then we prepared the hangi.

Those who know me well are aware of the enjoyment I derive from cooking food outside on or over a campfire. I have tried just about every method known to man but, until then, I had never seen the Maori hangi. Peter had the special volcanic rocks required still buried from the previous party, and he unearthed them. The principle is simple enough. A deep trench is dug (the one used previously is taboo; a fresh plot has to be selected). It is filled to the top with kindling and thick logs, and a great heap of rocks is piled on top of them. The fire is lit in the bottom of the trench and is allowed to burn for several hours. As it burns down, the rocks become incredibly hot and fall into the trench. They are then removed, the trench is cleared of ash and charcoal and the clean hot rocks are replaced.

Meanwhile, meat of several kinds (in our case pork, lamb and two turkeys) is packed into a big wire basket on a bed of watercress, and surrounded by potatoes, onions, carrots, celery, mushrooms and anything else available. It is covered with a clean, wet cloth and covered again by several wet sacks before being placed into the hellish pit. Then all the loose earth is piled on top and the whole lot completely sealed. Any escaping steam is stopped by yet another divot of earth and a careful watch is kept for (in our case) about five hours when the whole lot is carefully retrieved.

Neighbours came from far and near to partake of our fare and I could see that, although wasteful in terms of fuel on a small scale, the hangi is an ideal method of cooking for a large outdoor gathering. Everything was tender and well cooked. None of the flavours had been lost, and I remember the occasion with great pleasure.

With turkey livers and necks in the makeshift tackle bag, Peter and I went eel fishing in one of the many wide streams a few miles distant. It had been in flood recently and a big eddy swirled near to our bank.

"Here is where I caught a 25-pounder last year," said Peter. "They'll be lining up to be caught."

I put a big chunk of liver onto a size 2 hook and tossed it out to the edge of the eddy.

"Too far," said Peter.

"It'll swing round," I replied.

The rod tip nodded.

"Definitely an eel bite," said Peter. "Give it a bit of time."

A slow, decisive pull developed at that precise moment and I prepared to do battle with an eel. I had on a multiplier loaded with, I believe, 14lb test line. On reflection it might have been 20lb. Either way the idea was not to give a big eel a chance!

The line, however, was suddenly slack and, accepting a missed chance with a shrug, I began retrieving. A silver shape leapt clear of the water in the middle and the line tightened as a rainbow took up the slack. It jumped again and again as I gained control, and when it came towards the bank Peter wallowed through the mud and into the eddy. Here was something neither of us had expected, and he was not about to miss the opportunity. The fish weighed about 3lb and obviously had little to say for itself on such gear, which was

a pity. It was the first and the best of five which, for some reason, decided that wild turkey liver was flavour of the month.

I dressed them out on the spot and next day six of us, including Peter and his lovely wife Diane, enjoyed some of the fillets dressed up in a cheese sauce. The rest I left in the freezer to be enjoyed later in my absence.

It was not until I had left the country that Peter informed me my fish had been caught illegally!

Less than two years later I lay in the Australian bush, counting the southern stars that for ever confuse me, before drifting into a sound sleep beneath the scented eucalyptus. I dreamed (it seemed like the whole of the long night through) about Peter and of New Zealand. I have no idea why it happened so. Life had been of the very best on that particular trip and I had been glad to find the escape I needed from the hustle and bustle of town life. I had completed my travel schedule and had no thoughts of any more flying until my return to the United Kingdom, but it seemed that New Zealand was calling me once more. What followed was somewhat strange. I returned from my bush trip to be greeted by my wife who suddenly expressed the desire to take a side trip.

She is a seasoned traveller but does not particularly enjoy the hassle of passport control, baggage handling, customs or immigration checks. This trip, she had assured me, was going to be a simple London–Perth–London schedule. What made her change her mind? Why did her decision coincide with my outback dreams?

I will never know. She simply suggested that we should "pop over to see Peter and Diane".

A trip of that kind involves crossing the Australian continent to Sydney and then on to Auckland. From Auckland to Te Kuiti is a long drive in a hired car, which has to be collected at the airport, and I remembered, from previous occasions, that New Zealand does not really come to life until the rest of the world is up and going. After an all-night flight from Perth, I expected, and experienced, a long, long, wait until the hire car company clerk turned up for work! "Popping over to see Peter and Diane" took us about twelve hours but it was worth it. Air fares had hit rock bottom, we had enjoyed an excellent flight on Air New Zealand, and we were assured of a welcome at Peter's old farmhouse. I was thrilled to be back to improve my education, and perhaps even more so to hear Diane inform me that the "kitchen's all yours for the next two weeks".

It was easy to understand her attitude. *She* knew I loved to cook. I knew that New Zealand was a pot hunter's paradise and that Peter was a true pot hunter. I envisaged a period of full and plenty. Wild goat, pig, turkey and rabbit were there for the taking. So, too, were eels and trout.

I have often said that trout fishing in New Zealand is not as simple as the Tourist Authorities suggest, and I do not believe the stocking programmes there compare with our own. Nevertheless, no-one should ever go fish hungry, and there are compensations.

"Have you ever eaten 'possum?" asked a young visitor to the farm. I replied that, so far, I had not, and we struck a deal.

Peter would shoot one (in fact he came back within twenty minutes with the body), I would dress it and he would cook it next day. Opossum in cream sauce is delicious!

Again Peter and I went eel fishing and I found myself actually filleting a couple of 4-pounders. It was my own idea and I found it much easier than traditional gutting and skinning. I learned that there are, in fact, two skins on an eel and that both are easily stripped from a long fillet. We ate them cooked several different ways and enjoyed them all.

I have hunted much quarry with Peter over the years but it was fishing that brought us together.

They say that fishing is a great leveller, but I think there is a lot more to it than that.

It is a builder of friendships.

In a long fishing life, which has involved much travel, I have seen many friendships develop. That with Peter has been one of the special ones.

Whether I shall ever see him again remains in the lap of

the gods. I know that I will never go to New Zealand without spending time with him. I know the welcome will be there. And, in the unlikely event that he ever comes to the UK, he knows the same applies.

22
TOMMY

Tommy and I were serving soldiers towards the end of the war in Europe and I had just returned from France when we met. In those days sporting fishers and shooters were regarded as a little odd by most other army personnel and to meet another "nut-case" was like a breath of fresh air to both of us. He was an experienced wildfowler. I knew nothing of estuary shooting but could usually bowl over a rabbit or a hare for the pot. We were both keen coarse fishers but had little in the way of tackle. We had no money to speak of but in those days it would not have helped. Fat wallets could not have purchased fishing rods or nets or lines. None was available in the shops. A few fly hooks and eel hooks were available here and there and, very occasionally, we were able to buy a box of cartridges. A whole box! Twenty-five opportunities which we used to full advantage without being too sporting!

"Don't be nice about it," Tommy would say. "It's grub we want, not sporting shots."

We became adept at stalking quarry and I remember many long cycle rides through snow and floods across Pilling Sands with rabbit, hare, duck or pheasant hanging on the handlebars as we took our quarry home to our new and meat-hungry wives.

Those unofficial overnight "passes" were usually planned to coincide with our having quarry to spare. We shared a hare

169

occasionally because we were lucky enough to be billeted where there were plenty to spare. It is to our credit, I believe, that we settled for one on many occasions when we might easily have killed two.

I taught Tommy how to call hares and, to be honest, most of those we shot were "sitters", but we were faced with lean times.

Night after frozen night he and I squatted on the marshes in greatcoats and "Forces-comfort" balaclavas (knitted by loving old ladies and issued to unappreciative "squaddies" as part of the war effort) waiting for the sound of geese, mallard and widgeon. Once in a while we would be in the right place at the right time but there were many nights of cold frustration. I remember them still today and wonder how those old ammunition boots stood up to it. Perhaps, even more so, I wonder how our wet and frozen feet survived it all. I will have no more of it! I gave up marsh wallowing many years ago but I believe those days with Tommy made me a better hunter in the true sense of the word.

At one stage we shared an old muzzle loading piece which must have been unbelievably dangerous. When I think of the mixed powders and the different-sized shot we shovelled into that long, rusty, old barrel, I marvel that we survived. We were surely in more danger than the quarry we sighted!

Nevertheless it served us well, as did the fully choked, single-barrelled, hammer gun we also owned.

We were able, at the time, to get rabbit snares cheaply and, since we were surrounded by rabbits, we took advantage of those we accumulated. Our excursions took on an air of secrecy and our comrades wondered why we were later in bed and still up very early in the morning. We feared that, if they knew our secrets, they might have demanded "some of the action" but, in fact, we need not have worried. None was interested in early rising for sporting purposes and our "game larder" in the old potting shed remained undiscovered by everyone except the local poacher who knew about it but would never have betrayed us.

When we fished the local ponds with our improvised rods

and strong sewing thread lines, we caught roach, bream and perch, which we usually returned. We ate a meal of bream once and although the flesh was edible with no hint of mud, we found the bones too much of a problem.

We also caught eels, however. Not the usual, small boot-lace but fine eels up to almost 3lb apiece. It took Tommy a while to accept that they were edible but, once convinced, there was no stopping him. He developed a passion for eels and there were many times when we caught, cooked and ate them by the waterside. A sprinkling of salt and a square of fence wire-netting laid over campfire embers saw them cooked to a turn. There was a period during summer when we would deliberately set forth with the necessary salt and bread intending to indulge in an eel supper. We lived, per-haps, in a fantasy world but I doubt if we were ever any the worse off for our indulgence. Nor, I am sure, was anyone else. The future was still uncertain. The Far East was still to be conquered and those were stolen hours of magic!

I still have no idea how Tommy acquired the dog! He just turned up with it one day saying that it had taken a fancy to him. It was of many mixed breeds and a lovable rascal with, we discovered later, a positive instinct for hunting. Our walks along the hedgerows had until then been casual affairs. We went always hoping to kick up a rabbit or to stalk one and take a pot shot but Tommy had always insisted we needed a dog. It is not easy to conceal a dog in a military detachment but Tommy managed it. He was a fitter and there was room in the big barn that had been converted into a workshop. Cookhouse scraps provided by almost everyone connected with the small detachment made certain that there was no possibility of the hound ever suffering from hunger pains.

"How do you know he will hunt?" I asked Tommy soon after he acquired the dog.

"Pick up that gun and watch him," Tommy replied. I did so and the dog all but turned somersaults in excitement. I took him out into the neighbouring field, pointed to the hedgerow and said, "Hi lost". He dived into the thicket and began to hunt. Tommy and I were sure we had "cracked it" and it has to be said that our game returns improved from that moment onwards. Tommy wasn't satisfied, however.

"What we need is a ferret," he announced.

"Wrong time of year for ferreting," I counselled. I had had a great deal of early experience with ferrets. Tommy had had *none* at all but he was adamant.

Percy, another local poacher, we were told, had one for sale. Tommy fashioned a hutch out of a large barrel and we struck a deal. In truth I believe Percy was glad to be rid of the creature. He was one of the old breed of hedgerow poachers who saw little sense in keeping a ferret for half a year without profit. In those days ferret kits were cheap and plentiful and it was common practice to buy fresh stock at the start of each season.

Ferreting in summer is not generally to be advised but there are years when hot and dry conditions deter adult rabbits from breeding. It is said that, without moisture, the does can produce no milk for their kits and recent years of experience in the Australian outback have convinced me of the truth of it.

The season when Tommy and I hunted summer rabbits with Fagan the ferret was a hot, dry and exciting one. We had no purse nets and were obliged to use valuable cartridges when the ferret bolted a rabbit — which it did well enough from time to time.

It was obvious that the dog (who never seemed to be given a name) had seen ferrets before and we experienced no problems when they hunted together. Mutual respect was the order of the day and Tommy always insisted that they had "a sniff of each other before starting work". He quickly became adept at handling and working with the ferret and despite the bad timing of the operation, he proved that we need never go meat hungry.

Summer moved on to autumn and then to winter proper and our cycle rides across the marsh became more hazardous as we fought floods and snows to reach our respective homes. After five years in the Middle East and a short spell in France, however, those stolen weekends were sheer magic for Tommy and me. Part of the magic, of course, was taking home freshly shot or caught game for our respective wives. He always insisted that those ladies "learned how to be proper housewives" as a result of our providing the where-withal. We spent an incredible Christmas Day once with guns, ferret and fishing rods while the rest of the detachment joined the Regiment for the celebrations. Stone cold sober, we listened to their tipsy ramblings with deep content later.

A few days afterwards, a brace of pheasants presented to the small Officers' Mess with our compliments secured an unofficial two-day pass for both of us! We had been missed at the Regimental Dinner and hints were dropped!

When, to our shame, we shot and failed to retrieve a dozen or so wild duck from the marsh because they landed in the river and were swept away downstream in the darkness, Tommy and I decided to build a boat! In the resident army workshop we worked with wood, canvas, nails and paint to make a horrendous punt. With it, we said, we would drift down to ducks in the manner of punt gunners and retrieve any birds we shot from the marsh. Little did we know!

The finished boat would not pass through the doors of the workshop and even after modification we were obliged to admit that without an army of volunteers we would never carry it to the marsh. And even if we did, how would we get it back? We abandoned our plans and set fire to the boat which, on reflection, would probably have sunk without trace in any event!

Shortly after that the ferret strangely disappeared from its quarters and it was whispered that Percy had been seen in the vicinity. Tommy and I had taken to meeting him in his local pub and telling him of our successes and failures from time to time. I am in no doubt whatsoever that Percy stole back his ferret but the time was rapidly approaching when our "easy number" had to end. A return to barracks prior to demobilisation was ordered and army discipline was resumed.

Tommy and I remained friends long after our return to civilian life and we talked of our experiences, particularly about our "lost cause" boat, when we fished for tench on Wotton Lakes some years later. It had been our only real failure. All our other ventures had succeeded well enough. We talked of our exploits as we picked our way across the marshes as responsible civilians and we never lost our love for pot hunting during the lean years of rationing.

It took a long time for news of Tommy's death to reach me but considering the fact that he ended his days in New Zealand, there is, perhaps, some excuse for my not knowing sooner. On the other hand, I had tried several times to catch up with him during my travels to the Antipodes.

He was, at one stage, in Western Australia but after tracking him down there I was told he had returned to Fleetwood. When I was next in Fleetwood some years later, I tried to find him again.

"He's gone to New Zealand to live," said a close relative. Murphy's Law had struck again. I had been in New Zealand myself only a few weeks earlier! Too early or too late has been the story of my life regarding a reunion with Tommy. Now, of course, it really is too late but I will always cherish the memories of his super-optimism during our sporting activities.

We were mature and experienced married men when we first met but I still think that in a way Tommy and I grew up together. Rest easy, mate!

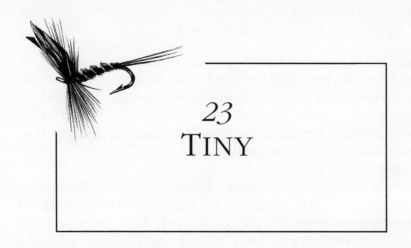

23
TINY

Bernard Venables wrote of Tiny Bennet, a bearded, grizzly voiced mountain of a man who, at 6′ 8″ tall, was a visual asset for the newly launched *Angling Times* (in 1953), that when he emigrated to Canada, "Canada took him to her transatlantic heart. His big ways had found their natural stage. Tiny quickly became a TV star of the great outdoors." All so very true.

I knew Tiny and his wife Joy as a result of a feature on tench fishing in which we all co-operated on Wotton Lakes in 1954. (Or was it 1955?)

I never kept in touch with him after that but my friends at *Angling Times*, in particular Circulation Manager Ken Sutton, kept me informed of his progress.

In 1967, when I decided to take my wife on a convalescent cruise to Canada and then on to the USA, I wrote to Tiny and reminded him of our early associations. He remembered at once and answered my letter in a very enthusiastic manner.

How long was I staying? How tight was my itinerary? I surely could not come to Canada without us meeting up again, and was I bringing my fishing tackle, and could I bring him some big sliding floats?

Such an invitation simply could not be refused and my wife and I eventually took the train from Montreal to Toronto where we were met by Tiny.

Some of our fishing trips have been recorded elsewhere

and I still have fond memories of our days at Waubaschene and on the French River. I remember more, however, the great exuberance of that big and generous heart. Tiny had the frame of a giant, the enthusiasm of a schoolboy and, as Bernard so aptly put it, the heart of a child. He declared that, had the outdoors not been great already, Tiny would have made it so.

When I first went to Canada I was a coarse fisherman pure and simple. I had become a carp fanatic after being involved for many years in the pursuit of tench from many different waters. I felt then that it was obscene even to consider killing fish for the table but I was soon to learn that Tiny did precisely that. When he went fishing, he expected to cook fish later. He had learned to accept the way of life on the great American continent. It hurt me at first to knock fish on the head or hitch them on to a stringer to keep them fresh, but I saw the logic of it in due course.

Tiny and I discussed the question of "catch-and-release" many times and I quickly realised that those discussions took on the form of a debate. We argued, it is true, but never, as far as I can remember, did we strive always to win.

"An argument or debate should be aimed at finding the truth," said Tiny. "The object is not to try and win at all costs."

Richard Walker had already made a similar statement to me on many occasions. Whether he was quoting Tiny Bennet or whether the reverse was true I have no way of knowing. I have to say, however, that of the two folk involved, Richard was more likely to break the golden rule. He argued to win if he was convinced that he was right. In so doing he would toss in "red herrings", misquote (deliberately) sayings, and invent statistics to fool the unwary. Tiny was well aware of this having worked with Richard many times but it has to be said that he talked of him often with affection.

It is far from easy for a coarse fish angler, who has been brainwashed into believing that all fish are sacred and that none should ever be killed, to conform to the customs of another country. Tiny told me that at first he had tried to re-educate Canada's fishing public into adopting "catch-and-release" principles but he had been quick to realise that there was not the slightest chance of him doing so.

Today, some 27 years later, there are signs of change. Some provinces now insist that barbless hooks are used at all times. Catch-and-release is not strictly mandatory but there is a saying going the rounds to the effect that anglers should "Eat all you can but return all you can't".

Those exact words were used by Tiny to me all those years ago to discourage the carting away of large stringers of prime walleye, pike, bass and crappie. He was on a loser when it came to releasing carp simply because Canadians had (and still have, it seems) a hatred for them. The carp he caught regularly were released quietly and without fuss. It was better, he said, not to be seen as a carp lover.

Nevertheless, it was he who first showed me how to flllet a carp and prepare it in the style best known to Americans of the middle-west. He also told me (but did not demonstrate it) of the method used to prepare carp for smoking.

I confess to a feeling of near-nausea when I first saw a fillet knife go into the back of a prime common carp to dislodge many of those great scales as it followed the rib cage. When the fillets were completed and the offal and skin were discarded, however, there was little or nothing to distinguish the flesh from that of many other kinds of fish.

The process of "scoring", i.e. making a number of cuts very close together both vertically and horizontally to reduce the bones to insignificant scraps, was among the first of Tiny's lessons to this unbeliever. Eating smoked and fried carp in various parts of the American continent has since become common practice.

I now know, of course, that Tiny was right all those years ago. He chose either to release his carp or (on the odd occasion) take it for the table. He insisted that there was nothing sinful about eating any freshwater fish. What was obscene, he maintained, was killing fish and NOT eating them.

He fitted into Canada. He accepted Canada's lifestyle and principles but he could never forgive those so-called sportsmen who shot spawning carp with bows and arrows and left them to rot on the bank. He was not so much against the bow-hunting because he knew that there was an unlimited harvest to be reaped and that carp could never be over-cropped. He cringed in the manner of all decent sportsmen, however, at the thought of subjecting prime fish to such cruel indignities. His remarks on the subject were to the effect that if you had no intention of eating it, why kill the creature at all.

I have always felt that way. Where there is a superabun-dance of quarry, a regular harvest is in order. That is why, when Tiny and I fished up on the French River for a week, we lived largely on the walleye we caught daily. Such fish as bass and pike were returned for the simple reason that they were not exactly prolific. It may well have been a change for us to have sampled other fish but we were happy with the abundance of easy-to-catch walleyes. Those shore lunches we enjoyed on the banks of the French River were the first I had ever experienced, apart from the ghastly concoctions my friends and I conjured up as kids along the banks of the River Thame. Roach, perch, eels, gudgeon and even small bream ended up in our big frying pan in those early days. They were not to be compared with the fish meals provided by our Indian guide but I could not help being reminded of them.

Most of my friends are aware that I enjoy cooking out of doors and that I tend to take over the cooking chores in a communal camp situation. This is because I always had to do it in self-defence in the early 'fifties when my comrades at the waterside set out to ruin every item of good food in sight! They did it deliberately!

I feel sure, however, that my days and nights with Tiny encouraged me to get back to campfire basics and to revel in the joys of food cooked to perfection in true, primitive style.

I recall that Tiny and I had a boat to ourselves on a vast expanse of water somewhere in Ontario. I swear I captured it all on 8mm film but I cannot remember the actual location. Almost certainly it was somewhere on or around Lake Ontario. I remember that the day was hot, the water was inviting and that we both swam in the nude while our shore lunch fire (which we were handling ourselves) burned through to make hot coals. We wrapped our fish fillets (there were several different kinds) in foil and tossed them on the coals while we dried off in the sun. I remember that we gorged ourselves and finally stretched out in the sun on that hard gravel bank. Sheer bliss. Unashamed luxury – until the mosquitoes started to attack! That is another lesson I learned in the company of Tiny Bennet. Never venture out into the Canadian bush without some kind of insect repellant!

My visit with Tiny was all too brief but I felt, at the end of it, that he had become a true friend. I felt, too, that we had a great deal in common, that our approach to life in general was on the same wavelength.

Tiny is no longer with us. Big, in his case, was not enduring. I cannot remember the year of his death but I will remember always so many facets of his big-hearted, happy-go-lucky life. I could tell a thousand stories – and perhaps one day I will – but, for the time being, I feel privileged to have known him and to have learned so much from his laid-back philosophy.

Tiny never taught me anything about how to catch fish. He never tried to; he never believed he could. He did, however, teach me a little about life itself. The great outdoors became greater under his guidance and my own great love of it became even greater as a result of having known him!

24
MACK

There was (and probably still is) a length of rocky coastline at Sidi Bishr in Egypt where the sea water lashed the cliff face and sent a spout of water shooting up through a hollow "chimney". The fishing in that area was particularly good and it was there that I met Mack – another soldier. He was talking earnestly to a friendly Arab who had apparently lent him his spare cane pole. Both were catching fish by using some kind of beetle for bait. The fish were strong little fighters. They were edible but their dorsal fins held some kind of poison. As I found out later.

I was intrigued, to say the least. Mack was the first person I had met out there to show any interest in fishing. We compared notes and became friends. The Army moves in mysterious ways and, in due course, Mack and I found ourselves in the same unit.

We spent long days and nights waiting for the war to happen in that godforsaken desert and, although, for the most part, I hated it all, I have often wondered if my five-year stint caused me to become the true lover of the outdoors I am today. I now revel in the opportunity to "lose" myself in the wilderness anywhere in the world.

While we waited, we hunted. Mack was a superb pistol shot and a field sportsman of considerable skill. He spoke lovingly of the city but he had obviously spent much time in Scotland's countryside. He was undoubtedly a survivor and could read the tracks left by the jack rabbits of the Libyan desert with a degree of certainty. Those vast expanses of scrub looked very much alike to me but Mack seemed to know where to hunt. He snared one rabbit with a piece of throttle cable. I managed once to kill one with my improvised catapult but Mack, on occasions, shot them fairly consistently with a looted Italian .32 automatic. He could sense the outline of a squatter and would creep slowly forward to get in range. He missed more than once but, of course, one only remembers the hits.

Those tough old carcases really needed stewing but, for the most part, we did our best with the frying pan. Whatever else, they were preferable to bully beef, and a few other comrades were happy to share our bounty.

It was Mack who dreamed up the idea of making fishing rods from tank aerials. We were leaguered close to the coast at one stage and small parties were allowed to go to the sea for a daily swim. Mack found a rocky bay where we could dangle our lines into the quiet water. We caught very few fish but expected none at all. Lying there half-naked, soaking up the sun and playing at fishing was a great joy after some of the harder times.

"All we need now," said Mack, "is a bottle of good Scotch whisky. This would then be heaven on earth."

Most of my desert memories are now vague. I can no longer remember dates and times – even to the year – but I do recall one place and one experience which I shared with Mack. I was never allowed to forget it.

We had been detailed to take a big truck from (I believe) Alexandria to somewhere north of Mersa Matruh. As dusk approached we pulled up, cooked a meal, rolled out our blankets and settled on the sand for the night. I remember that the night was cold and that Mack snored for most of it.

When we roused at dawn I pumped up the tank stove to brew tea and Mack pulled on his shorts. A monstrous scorpion, objecting to the disturbance of his slumber, took evasive action after biting him in a particularly fleshy part.

I noted that the spider was black and, despite conflicting

advice offered on the subject, felt obliged to help. Mack, I thought, would have done the same for me!

So, after stamping on the wretched creature, I performed what all squaddies reckoned to be the proper treatment for black scorpion stings. I cut the tiny wound with a razor blade and sucked and spit until I was sure the venom was extracted.

Mack was suitably grateful but I swear he really saw the whole episode as a joke.

He looked down at the dead spider and quoted "Wee sleekit, cow'ring tim'rous beastie – serves ye blanking well right!" He suffered no ill effects. I doubt if he ever thought he would!

From then on, however, if we had any kind of disagreement, he would shrug his shoulders, put on a wide grin and, in his best American accent, whisper "Kiss my butt".

I lost touch with Mack some years ago and have no way of knowing whether he is still alive.

I heard once that he was working as a bailiff on one of Scotland's smaller game rivers and that he was, in fact, teaching fly casting as a spare-time activity.

I had a letter from him some twenty years ago, telling me that he was going to join his family somewhere in the Antipodes. I forget just where.

He signed the brief missive,

"Your old mate from the blue*
Spider Mack (K.M.B.)"

* Blue meaning desert in squaddie terms.

25
ZEKE

I cannot remember exactly when I first met Zeke. All I can say is that I know it was in Arkansas and that I saw him as the ultimate male chauvinist. He was almost 80 years old and he told me he fished every day in the summer and hunted rabbits, quail and other game all winter. Most days he would sit under the same shady tree, cane pole in a forked stick, cooler box of iced beer by his side, and his fishing line looped around a bare, big toe. He never cared very much whether his "big gob o' nite crawlers" (bunch of worms) was taken or not, but he seldom retired fishless, according to the locals. He preferred the creek to the lake near his home but every so often he would decide to "go for a lunker". That meant that he was going to "set a spell" and wait for a big carp or catfish to fall for his chicken liver bait.

"Carp's good eatin' " he assured me once, and proved it on another occasion by letting me taste a portion of a hot-smoked 10-pounder. It had an exceptional flavour and encouraged me to consider harvesting a few for myself later.

Zeke, on the day in question, had set up his tackle outside the small cafe in the Beaver Lake Dock area. This was a floating construction and served to supply passing boats with food, soft drinks, gasoline and fishing baits. Zeke had set up his tackle on the wooden deck. His bait was in the water about 30 feet out and his line was taut to his rod tip.

Every carp angler in the United Kingdom knows that you

do not, or should not, keep a tight line situation where carp are the quarry. Carp tend to race off with the bait and rods are apt to follow if they are not secured. All carp anglers of my acquaintance make provision for passage of line by opening the bale arm of the reel. That way, the carp can proceed without feeling any resistance when the line peels off the spool. It is common sense and nothing more. I noticed, however, that Zeke's bale arm was closed and his rod, far from being secure, was lying on the board structure. It was none of my business but I had to ask, since he was perched upon a kitchen chair with his rod lying well out of reach.

"How on earth are you going to strike a carp if you get a hit?" I asked. (Americans get "hits"; they do not get "bites", "takes" or "runs".) Zeke raised his foot and held it poised over his rod.

"I'll just lift up m' foot and stomp on it," he replied.

And while his foot was poised about 6 inches above his tackle, some unknown carp decided to hit the bait. Zeke's stomp was half a second too late! His foot hit the boards as the rod did a horizontal take-off into the deep waters of Beaver Lake! To the best of my knowledge it was never seen again, but Zeke was unconcerned. He knew where to pick up a replacement!

He had a small, general store which also sold bait, tackle and cheap rods to visitors to the area. It would never have served a customer at all had it not been for his patient wife who carried on the business while he pursued his sporting activities. Life, for Zeke, was too precious to waste at work!

We asked him once if he would tell us how he managed to do it. How did he get away with it? Fishing all day, every day, without so much as a peep from his patient and loving wife? If there was a secret it might prove useful to us, we thought. And one day, while the sun shone and the insects hummed, and the catfish were taking better than usual, old Zeke told us.

When he was young, he said, it was the custom for a bridegroom to hire a horse and buggy to take his bride to the honeymoon cabin after the wedding ceremony, and so, when he finally decided it was time to marry and settle down himself, he did much the same thing. At least, he hired the buggy but, instead of hiring the horse, he bought a beat-up nag from the local horse-trader whose stables apparently served as a half-way house for animals destined for the glue factory!

After the ceremony Zeke brought round the buggy, harnessed up the nag, helped his bride aboard and drove off to the accompaniment of best wishes from his friends and relatives.

A mile along the track the horse reared up at a rattlesnake almost upsetting the buggy, and Zeke grunted, "That's once."

A little further on, the old horse, tiring slightly, strayed off the track on to the rough and bumpy desert. The buggy filled with dust, Zeke's bride was nearly thrown out, and it was some time before the track was regained.

Zeke snarled, "That's twice."

When the honeymoon cabin was reached, Zeke alighted and was reaching up to help his bride down when the horse backed up and rolled the wheel over his foot. Zeke said, "That's it. That's three times," and promptly shot the old horse through the head with his big 45!

His bride was horrified. "Honey," she said, "that was just horrid of you to do that to that poor old horse."

And Zeke looked her squarely in the eyes and said, "That's once!"

"Ain't never had another peep out of her since then," he assured me with a twinkle in his old blue eyes.

Somehow I think he might have been pulling a Limey's leg just a wee bit. But who cares? He was a great character, and a great fisherman in his own special way. I doubt if he will still be sitting under the same tree with his old, white panama hat shading his eyes from the sun when I next visit the USA, but I'm sure he'll be fishing somewhere. After all, St Peter was a fisherman and he could well be looking for a celestial carp fishing buddy! Couldn't he?

26
DERRICK

I met Derrick Davenport in the early 1950s and, although it is fair to say that we have not fished together for, perhaps, 40 years, I still regard him as a close friend. I also agree with the late Richard Walker who once referred to him as a "better angler than all us lot put together".

When Ken and Joe Taylor were fishing with me at Wotton Lakes, soon after World War II, the generally accepted lore of tench fishing went very much by the board. We specialised and were blessed with the opportunity to fish a remarkable and prolific tench lake. We caught a lot of quality tench, built up a reputation, and became known as The Taylor Brothers. That is when Derrick Davenport made contact.

"Sporting-wise," he wrote, "there is nothing to suggest that I am not a fit person to make your acquaintance and fish your waters, if such a possibility exists."

It was a letter from a specialist. An intelligent angler, a thoughtful person, and one whom I regarded as being of both interest and benefit to the small world in which we existed. The outcome was that Derrick joined us, fitted in with our plans, and learned a little from us while, at the same time, passing on to us an incredible amount of angling, common sense, dedicated thinking *and* an ability that sometimes left us astonished.

We allowed him access to our big pontoon boat one day while we took part in a friendly competition on the lower lake. Later in the day he showed us 21 tench housed in our monstrous and roomy keep-sack. "They're not very big," he said, "but I've had a lot of fun."

They averaged about 3lb each and it was only then that we began to understand "swim production".

Had we three stalwarts fished it in his place, we might well have caught 21 tench between us! An average of seven per person. A great overall result but only modest in terms of individuality. Henceforth, when we all fished together, often from two anchored boats, Derrick would tell all and sundry that *we* had caught – say – 40 fish in the day. The fact that one of us (and this includes Derrick) had caught as many as the other three together was not of interest. It was *our* catch that counted and I have always admired Derrick for seeing it our way. The competition was always there (and it still is) but strictly between us and our quarry – the fish!

It has to be said, however, that all specialist anglers can tire of the same quarry. We were encouraged, as a result of Richard Walker's writings, to seek carp as being more demanding. Derrick took us to Wadhurst Lake and showed us the finer points of floating crust fishing. There was little to it really but such was his skill that he made it appear easier than it was. Here was a man who could cast a sodden crust to the surface of the distant rushes and be accurate to an inch. Well – so could we! Big deal! The only difference, however, was that he could do it with his left hand just as easily as with his right! You think that is not impressive? Come on!!

Later, Derrick decided that carp were "big, fat and lumbering" and that he needed to seek quarry with a little finesse.

For some time he sought estuary mullet here and there. Later I went the same route – briefly and independently – and I quickly noted and understood his enthusiasm.

We all but burned him to death once on a small island in Hertfordshire. Richard Walker, replenishing a burnt-out cooking stove with meths, caused a sheet of flame to shoot across the campsite and Derrick was very badly burned.

"Dick," he yelled, "you *are* a wally!"

That was not strictly the word he used but, to his everlasting credit, having once made his protest, he *never* mentioned the incident again! He was treated in hospital and joined us in another week's fishing here and there before returning to his Hampshire home. He suffered but he never, at any time, complained.

I have to say that this, and his totally philosophical attitude, endeared him to us from that day forward!

The Russians launched a satellite some time later and it was obviously the media's main talking point.

"Satellite?" said Dick Walker. "Big deal. So what? Davenport was satellite (set alight) two years before the Russians even thought of it!"

It was a light-hearted cover-up for a serious mistake and Dick was the first to admit it.

"He's right! I was a wally" he said. "But at least he only ever told me once. He's forgotten it now but I never will!"

Nor did he! Every so often Dick would mention the event and remark upon Derrick's totally laid-back attitude.

There was one occasion when Dick stressed that attitude to perfection.

"I was about to say that Derrick Davenport was one of us," he declared. "On the face of it, however, he simply fits in with our line of thought. The truth is that Davenport's philosophy belongs on a plane that actually hovers well above ours. But he's still a mate and for that we must all give thanks."

Derrick Davenport has since become a worldwide traveller and a seeker of exotic fish. Many such fish are considered as being beyond the reach of the average angler, simply because the average angler is not prepared to seek out the possibilities of foreign fish pursuit.

The chances *are* there! Davenport has demonstrated the fact many times. It is simply a question of priorities and I have mine well documented. Like Davenport, I am prepared to save up my fishing time and fish once or twice a year in an area that is totally different from anything available in the UK. Like Davenport, I have discovered the great joys of seeking carp, catfish, white bass, sturgeon, smallmouth bass, walleye and goldeye along Manitoba's Red River. We shall *never* realise complete success but the truth, of course, is that we would not really wish to do so!

"Cold Comfort"

My very close and loyal friend Alec Martin deserves more than a chapter to himself and, one day, I'm sure, he will be truly recognised! Meanwhile, however, it is essential for me to say that he is deserving of more than this book's space can offer – and I am sorry for that.

It is a fact that one's closest friends, and most interesting colleagues, tend to be relegated in the never-ending search for space. But there is no great hurry. Time alone will tell and the full value of Alec's friendship will be aired in future works.

Without going into too much detail, I should explain that the 25-years' difference in our ages has enabled me to "pull rank" and demand a great deal of assistance in the field. Alec and I have fished, ferreted and pursued a number of different country pursuits together and my task, as a writer and TV participant, has been made easier by Alec's laid-back, I'll-do-this-for-you approach. I have always been grateful. I hope I have indicated that to him and I hope this special partnership will continue. We are both more-or-less fanatic campers and when I suggested he join me on one or two of our desperate "cold camps" in Canada, I was thrilled when he accepted.

There is more to camping in severely cold conditions than first meets the eye. It is fun. It is a special affair and I have to make the point that camping under canvas at temperatures down to minus 25°C is not to be regarded lightly. Warmth is of the utmost importance. A big camp-fire for both cooking and comfort has to be kept burning by day. At night, a big candle-in-a-jar at the foot of each bed helps to keep the five or six campers snug. But what about calls of nature? Who wants to venture out of the outfitter's tent in the early morning hours to "spend a penny"? Not us! We were too wise for all that. We each had our own "comfort" bottle. These wide-necked, screw-top bottles once held some kind of softener for machine-washed clothes. The trade name "Comfort" fitted the bill and we referred to them as such.

"Would it not be a good idea to tape up Alec's comfort bottle?" asked Stuart one morning.

I swear, hand-on-heart, I disagreed!

"That," I said, "would be a low-down trick to play on a colleague."

Nevertheless, Alec's bottle was securely taped and remained so until he needed it in the early morning hours. I was awakened by shouts of fierce abuse, oaths and curses as Alec struggled. So were the other campers. Those curses turned to genuine laughter in due course. I'm sure Alec enjoyed the joke too. In any event, he took it in true sporting fashion.

Then came the warning!

"Revenge will be mine," he swore. "You have merely awakened the sleeping giant!"

The following summer, Stuart and I airmailed a small taped-up cola bottle to Alec's home in Northampton. The instructions read "In emergency, tear, cut, rip, gouge, saw or chisel off the cap. If all fails – wet the bed!"

Inside the bottle I put an English fiver and suggested Alec indulge in a modest bottle of red wine.

He telephoned us in Canada later. The package had arrived with the early Monday-morning post and had dispelled his Monday morning blues entirely. It had made his day, he told us. So much so, in fact, that he was no longer in a revengeful mood. We were forgiven.

Stuart didn't believe him. Nor, to this day, do I!

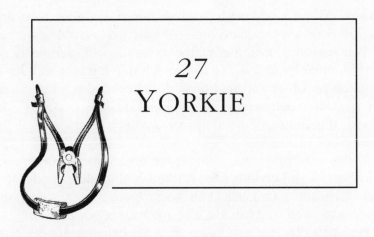

27
YORKIE

They called him Yorkie in the army but I still do not know exactly where he lived in civilian life. Except that it was "somewhere up north". He talked with a north-country accent but, unlike a few other Yorkshiremen I have met in a long lifetime, he did not claim to know everything about every subject under the sun. Perhaps it has been my misfortune to meet so many "know-alls" but that does nothing to ease the irritation I experience in their company!

Yorkie was a private soldier with no ambition other than to "get out of this bloody army and get back to living a life of my own". In many respects we were of a similar mould. As a young soldier I really had no thoughts about promotion and when I was involved in the push-and-pull of the Western Desert campaign my thoughts were mainly of survival at any cost.

We spent some long and boring spells in rat holes waiting for the war to begin (and praying for it to end), and Yorkie and I met up on odd occasions as a result of Army personnel juggling. There was a time, a very brief period, when we were part of the same tank crew. It was not a particularly exciting or frightening time and for much of it we were frustrated because of the inactivity. Do not misunderstand me. Neither of us was keen to "load up the cannon and take on the foe". We were no more cowardly than any of our comrades but we could see no point whatsoever in charging around a vast and totally useless desert in order to claim victory over a few square miles of sand and scrub!

Yorkie and I lost many fine comrades in that land of despair and desolation. We always felt that it might well have been either of us and that those lost lives did nothing at all for freedom, democracy, the Union Flag, the peace of the world, the future of mankind or anything else covered by politicians' platitudes.

Yorkie was a poacher, a dog lover, a survivor, a hunter and harvester of the countryside. It irked him to sleep under the stars beneath a tank sheet in wild open spaces where no game was seen to exist. He, like me, was a pot hunter.

He had a rifle that was taken from the Italians after the capture of General Electric Whiskers and his column outside Benghazi. Like the one I had looted, it was accurate. Very few Italian rifles were! We also had catapults made from ordinary pliers (to make the prongs) and elastic cut in thin strips from captured enemy vehicle inner tubes. The power required to pull back those slings was enormous but, once released, the ball-bearing missiles went with the speed of a bullet. Yorkie and I discovered that jack rabbits were present at one of our many Western Desert leaguers and we set out each evening to "walk up" our game. We had a yen for something other than bully beef stew, which was our regular evening meal. Make no mistake about it, we did not complain!

Yorkie took on the task of feeding six of us after dark each evening. His rations comprised bully beef, hard tack biscuits, onions (which somehow or other seemed to come up regularly with the rations), potatoes (tinned or otherwise), water (which was always scarce), salt, pepper and whatever else was available.

He cut a four-gallon petrol can in half, cleaned it up and used it to concoct our evening meal. When we captured a truckload of Italian tomato purée, cases of Italian milk and about a million Italian cigarettes, Yorkie was ahead of the looting patrol! We were living very "high on the hog" when our stews were cooked in milk and tomato purée rather than rationed water! We all smoked at the time and since we had not seen a cigarette ration for months (despite what the papers back home reported!) we settled for the captured stock. Any fag to a British Tommy was better than no fag at all! Eventually we became used to the taste and did not enjoy the real thing when it became available.

Yorkie schemed night after night to shoot one of the jack rabbits we saw from time to time in the scrub. He packed his captured rifle with "shots" cut from bullets in the hope that he could use it shotgun-style. The story has already been told how I went one better (as I thought) and adapted a Verey light pistol cartridge to fire several ounces of very unstable "shot". The result was alarming. The jack rabbit escaped and I "went back to the drawing board".

Nevertheless, I did manage to kill a jack rabbit with my catapult on one occasion and that night our bully beef stew was supplemented by jack rabbit portions!

Later, a gunnery instructor shot a gazelle with my well-oiled and very accurate Italian rifle, and six of us enjoyed venison for a couple of evenings. No big deal on the face of it but something very special at the time!

Our tank lost a track in one of the skirmishes and later a "big-end-knock" sent us back to the nearest repair depot where we waited with a group of other Royal Armoured Corps men for the engine to be reconditioned. Yorkie produced a pack of cards and, of all things, a ludo game complete with counters, dice and board. We had fashioned a bivouac out of tank sheets and were at once self-contained with several other comrades. They did not know us but they welcomed us at once. The unacceptable face of war undoubtedly brought out the best in those involved in it! If only such spirit could be encouraged to reappear today!

Yorkie was undoubtedly the ludo champion of the detachment. Luck or blinding skill with the counters put him well in front of all challengers. Large sums of money (much of it totally imaginary) were gambled on his last throws of the dice. Loud cheers echoed across the desert in the early morning hours as late-night games developed into all-night sessions.

It is hard to believe, some 50 years on, that sweaty,

unshaven, dusty and half-naked British soldiers might be seen cheering on their fancies in games of ludo, night after chilly, desert night! But that is how it was during the desert campaign.

In the darkness of the early morning hours, I was once awakened by a soft voice compelling me to listen but not to respond loudly. It was an urgent voice. A hoarsely whispered voice. A voice that belonged to Yorkie and, as such, was entitled to a hearing. I lay perfectly still and asked to be informed of the problem.

"Next bed to you," said Yorkie. "Old Mac's got a bloody great snake lying across his neck. It's thin but it's long. It may be poisonous and it may not. What in God's name can we do? If we startle him it may bite. If we don't he'll go potty in the morning if he sees it. Assuming he's not already dead from snakebite already."

Here was a problem indeed. The snake was still. Mac was breathing softly and in a deep sleep.

"Perhaps," said Yorkie, "if you spoke quietly, ever so quietly, and called his name repeatedly he might wake up without panic."

I agreed. "Let's both whisper his name until he comes to," I said. "Then we can warn him without causing any alarm."

We both began to whisper loudly, "Mac, Mac, Mac, wake up Mac."

It took some time but eventually Mac grunted that he was awake and listening. "Now listen, Mac," said Yorkie. "Don't, under any circumstances, react to this. Just lie still where you are and think out the problem carefully. Do you understand?"

Mac gave a grunt and indicated that he understood.

"Well," said Yorkie, "there's a bloody great long snake lying across your neck and ..." The remainder of his advice was lost to all concerned as Mac gave vent to a wild scream that awakened everyone within earshot. The bedclothes went in one direction, Mac went in another, and the thick, wire cable, that provided our bivouac with light via a series of tank batteries, stayed more or less where it was. The "snake" was no more than a length of that very cable which, in the half-light, had appeared to be putting a comrade's life at risk!

Yorkie never really lived it down and Mac never admitted to being really scared. We who were present, however, knew differently.

Yorkie and I went our different ways before going back to England prior to the D Day landings. I have not heard of him, or from him, to this day but if he reads this (as well he might with a hint of luck) I hope he will remember me with affection as I remember him.

He was not a particularly good soldier but, on reflection, nor was I. In fact, very few of us were.

He was, however, a survivor and a lover of wild and desolate places. That is what endeared him to me.

"I might get killed here tomorrow," he would say as he took a pull at his beer ration. "But I guess I'd just as soon die here in this godforsaken hole as anywhere else. At least, here, there's somewhere to run to for escape. You can't really say that about London or Liverpool or Lancaster, where the cathedrals stand in glory. I wonder, if the truth be told, which part *is* the most godforsaken?"

I cannot really say I agreed with Yorkie regarding all aspects of our life on Earth but I think I saw the point he was trying to make.

And even if I did not, and my thinking was all wrong, I'm sure I can rely on Yorkie to forgive me. He was, after all, that kind of person!

"Desert Song"

His rank was Captain and he was Chaplain to the troops in the besieged garrison of Tobruk. He was the only Padre I saw during my nine months stay but there may have been others. If there were, they, too, would have been called "Holy Joes" for that was the troops' title to all of that calling. The very term reeks of disrespect but, in fact, it was truly a term of endearment.

It fell my lot to drive Holy Joe to the extreme perimeters of the garrison in order that he might visit those wonderful Australian comrades who were dug-in between us and the enemy. I have to say that there was never a more ungodly situation than that outpost area!

I drove a 15 cwt. "bug" for the Padre. He left me while he paid his respects to those Aussies who were prepared to listen to him. (They were all respectful to him and welcomed his visit despite the fact that they would never have admitted it!)

I have been left in some very lonely and hostile situations in a long lifetime but I do not remember a more ungodly spot than that loathsome perimeter. My heart went out to those Aussie gunners but I felt aggrieved at being left with no protection in that particularly malicious situation. And I cursed Holy Joe. I cursed him and I told him I had done so on his return about two hours later!

"Did you really mean what you said?" he asked.

"Not really," I replied.

"Then I don't think it matters," said his Reverence.

On our return journey across that godless desert of sand, rocks, scrub, flies and intolerable sun, I tried to explain my own particular faith.

I had a tremendous faith, I insisted. But I found it hard to relate that to the pomp, splendour, gold and the opulent attitude of the Church.

Christ, I argued, was a poor man. What was the point of worshipping him by way of gold candlesticks, stained-glass windows and incense?

I truly had a strong faith. A very strong faith – which had helped me through the years (five in all) of the desert campaign, but I felt that the splendour of the church itself had little to do with *my personal* respect *for* my God. I am sure he understood!

On the other hand, I said, I loved the music of the popular hymns. I enjoyed singing them and I was convinced that some of the world's most beautiful music had its origins in simple Hymns of Praise.

What, he asked, was my favourite hymn? There was no hesitation on my part. As a lover of the countryside, I had always loved "The Harvest Hymn", "Come ye thankful people come: Raise the song of Harvest Home!"

Together, we drove across those miles of sand, rock, scrub and misery, singing "Come ye faithful" together and in harmony. It was truly joyous!

It could not have been less appropriate. Where could we look for, and hope to praise the Lord for, the harvest in this godless wilderness? And yet, somehow, it worked.

Holy Joe shook my hand when we parted. And I have to say that although the handshake in itself was totally alien to any normal relationship between officer and humble squaddie, it was recognised by us both.

I was uplifted by the experience. I am, truly, uplifted today every time I recall those precious hours.

28
UNCLE JOBEY

Uncle Jobey wasn't strictly an outdoorsman, but he was a keen fisherman and a pot hunter. He could shoot with a catapult as well as any man I knew, except my father, and he knew a thing or two about catching rabbits. I never knew him catch many fish of real note, but he had the blessed gift of enjoying his fishing. He was never short of a suitable excuse if he caught nothing, or if he failed to turn up on time. And he was a man with a store of stock phrases – most of which contained a hint of common sense. Above all, Uncle Jobey had a sense of humour that was in a class by itself. Some didn't quite understand it; others, like me, really enjoyed it.

"Why don't you take a walk along to the next lock, cross over, walk back and fish from the other bank?" he asked me one day when we were fishing the local canal together.

"Why?" I asked.

"Cos that's where you've been trying to cast all botherin' morning," snapped Uncle Jobey. He did not have a large swear-word vocabulary. Everything was "botherin'" to him.

He planned a big day on Tring Reservoirs some years ago. He had the bream weighed up, he was on holiday and he was going to enjoy showing all and sundry how it should be done.

"How did you get on then, Uncle Jobey?" asked my brother Ken on his return.

"If I had a bite, my cock, I never sin it," he replied.

(Everyone, but everyone, was "my cock" to Uncle Jobey!)

We took him, one very cold January morning, with the coach party to the River Ouse. It was a ghastly day of sleet and icy wind.

"Where's the nearest pub?" asked Uncle Jobey as noon approached.

"There's one 6 miles up the road," I said, "or there's one half a mile away on the other side of the river." And that, I thought, would quieten him until tea time. But not a bit of it.

Uncle Jobey went down to the shallows, removed his wellingtons, rolled up his trousers and waded across the upper Ouse. He was about 70 at the time, and there was ice on the margins.

At about 2.30 p.m., he returned, took off his boots and, again, waded the river barefoot.

"I never had a bite, my cock, but I had three lovely pints," he said when asked at the end of the day how he had fared.

It was our practice in those days, when fishing for tench or carp, to put up two rods in the hope of doubling our chances.

"That's no botherin' good," insisted Uncle Jobey. "If the fish are biting, two rods is too many. If they ain't, one's too botherin' many!"

It's hard to argue with logic like that! He was a great leg-puller and practical joker was our Uncle Jobey. He wound people's tackles in and attached odd items to them when they were temporarily absent from their pitch. And he told lies that were so obvious that no-one was expected to believe them.

"I saw the earth moving in between my taters tonight," he said one evening on his return from the allotments. "I went to the shed, grabbed a fork, waited till it moved again, and stabbed it."

"What was it," someone asked. "A mole?"

"No," said Uncle Jobey seriously. "It was a tater a-growin'."

We had a big old pontoon boat on Wotton Lakes in the 1950s, and Uncle Jobey asked if he and a friend might use it for a day.

"Of course," we told him.

At the best of times, with about 3 feet of free board, that pontoon was difficult to manoeuvre; in a high wind it was impossible. And it was windy on the day in question.

We had told Uncle Jobey to fish the "deep 'ole". It was marked, we said, by two prominent buoys and we explained where. About 300 yards south of the island.

"We got 'er to the deep 'ole, my cocks," he told us later, "but by the time we'd got the poles in to 'old 'er, we was back at the island again. We done that three botherin' times then we went 'ome!" I've felt like it myself many times.

He and his brothers were going ferreting one Sunday morning, so the story goes, and, since a long bike ride was involved, an early start was indicated.

"My alarm clock's busted," he said. "I can't be sure to wake up in time."

"No problem," said Jimmy (my father). "Tie a piece of string to your toe, leave it hanging out of the window and we'll give you a tug."

It so happened that Uncle Jobey woke in good time and was, in fact, standing up and about to start dressing, when the crew arrived. They saw the light on but they also saw the string moving and quietly pulled, pulled and pulled again.

And Uncle Jobey hopped and hopped until he reached the window on his untethered foot. Then, it is said, he swore loud and long until nearby dogs began barking and neighbours were roused from their Sunday morning slumbers.

I wouldn't say that Uncle Jobey was a good pike angler, but he went fairly regularly if he could get live baits. As a rule we of our generation caught all the baits for him. Somehow we were a bit quicker-on-the-draw when it came to hemp fishing for small roach. Or we thought we were. On reflection, I think perhaps his generation couldn't be bothered and praised our efforts highly for that reason only.

Halton Reservoir, in Bucks, was the scene of many of their piking activities and it is fair to say that in those days they had their share of fish.

Uncle Jobey fished one winter's day without a hint of a bite and finally gave up in the mid-afternoon. His can of live baits contained a number of corpses which, for some reason, after carefully releasing the remainder, he threw as far as he could out into the reservoir.

As each fish hit the water, it was taken quite positively and with a great swirl by a suddenly interested pike. Uncle Jobey's tackle was packed up and, since he had no more baits, he was powerless to do anything about it. But from that day on he had new ideas about pike fishing, which he expounded at every opportunity.

"If you don't get no bites on your live baits," he'd advise, "throw stones at your botherin' float. Stir 'em up a bit."

We took little notice and, in later years, when we developed the dead bait method, we seldom used floats for our pike fishing anyway.

But there was a time when Uncle Jobey's idea worked.

Dick Walker, my brothers and I were fishing an old canal in north Bucks for smallish pike because the nearby river was in flood. The water was clear and our small spoons had already taken several fish. One pike, however, plainly visible near the far bank, was simply lying still eyeing a rudd bait suspended from a traditional pike float.

It would not react; it looked very bored. Its body was tucked away in the rushes, its head poking out a yard or so from the bait.

I cannot remember who it was, but one of us quoted "Uncle Jobey's Law". And someone threw half a brick at the pike. It was a fair shot. The pike got out in a hurry and snatched the bait as it did so.

I do not believe I have ever witnessed anything quite so dramatic. One second the float was there, the next it had completely disappeared and the rod top was bending in an arc.

I cannot recall the size of the pike. I think it was a 6-pounder but I'm not sure. I am sure, however, that it was never going to come adrift. It had taken the bait with intent and not curiosity. Uncle Jobey was pleased when we told him.

"What did I tell you, my cocks?" he beamed. "You know I shan't tell you wrong when it comes to pike fishing."

Unlike my father and many others of his generation, Uncle Jobey was not strictly reliable. Whereas others insisted that punctuality was of the utmost importance, Uncle Jobey was somewhat laid-back at the thought. The importance of punctuality undoubtedly rubbed off and became almost an obsession with my brothers, cousins, friends and me. It has remained so until this day and I refuse to wait for anyone who is late. I do not expect them to wait for me. Uncle Jobey, however, saw things in a different light. We often met at crack of dawn to go fishing together but I was never surprised to be left waiting. I learned quickly not to wait too long and I knew exactly what the answer to my challenge would be later in the day. It was always the same.

"I got up, my cock, and I looked out of the window but that looked like rain so I went back to bed!"

We had a favourite fishing spot on the River Thame known as "The Meeting of the Waters"; a grand title for the spot where two small streams met. There was a quick walk to it but for some odd reason, Uncle Jobey always took the longer route. It puzzled me since I had been raised, as a very young child, along those very banks. I knew every mushroom patch, every crabapple tree and every hazelnut hedgerow for miles, and it seemed illogical to me to walk farther than necessary. Father solved the riddle.

"It's because the short walk takes you past his favourite wild damson tree," he said. "Jobey reckons that belongs to him and he strips it every year at the right time."

I confess I had never noticed the tree myself but, from then on, I studied form and, early one August morning, after a night shift in the bakery, I beat Uncle Jobey to it! Those damsons were superb! I never confessed and I have tried to keep the tree as *my* secret ever since. Over the years it has produced fruit for many gallons of wine and many jars of preserve.

Uncle Jobey was indeed a very good gardener and he produced an annual crop of vegetables from his allotment up until his death at the age of 83.

207

Onions, he insisted, were the most important vegetable of all.

"You can't cook nothing without onions," he insisted. "Well, anyway, my Nelly needs 'em," he said, referring to his wife, my aunt. "I reckon, if she b'iled my shaving water, she'd put an onion in it!"

I can still see him today, with his pint of ale in the local club, his spotless white "choker" over his immaculate shirt collar. I can still hear him insisting that "you young-uns know nothing about field sports" and I realise that I am now in the same spot myself.

Whether he was right or wrong is neither here nor there. The fact remains that I have to have a dig at the young-uns myself occasionally. And when they get to my age they'll probably be doing the same thing themselves. Life's like that!

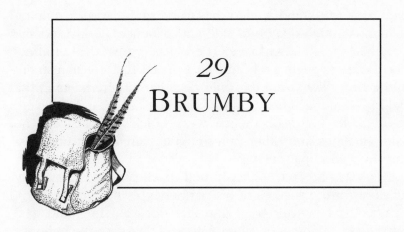

29
BRUMBY

Brumby was, without doubt, a poacher who walked by night to reap his harvests of game but he was never a profit-seeker. He swore, hand on heart, that none of the hares, rabbits, duck or pheasant he acquired were ever sold for cash. He was a generous soul who loved children and was ever willing to share bounty with friends and relatives who had growing families. It was rare, in the circumstances, for him to have a surplus but when he had one he would trade with the local butcher. A small joint here, a plate of liver or a dish of stewing beef there were good enough exchanges for a string of rabbits or a sack of mallard.

He was a good shot and had permission here and there to shoot pigeon and rabbits but there was more to his occasional forays than the shooting. As he walked the hedgerows and skirted the coverts he was invariably checking the lie of the land for some future night-time venture. Whenever the local Hunt met, he posed as a follower along with the rest and gained access by day to areas otherwise denied him. He could run a long net single-handed and with a speed and silence which belied his plump frame. He had a mongrel bitch which he called "Pickles" because, he said, there were 51 varieties in her pedigree. She sat while the net was set and on command went off to a far point before quartering the field back to the net driving fleeing rabbits ahead of her. She was, Brumby said, "a natural". He had obviously trained her well to her task and while it has to be said that such training demands a high degree of skill and patience, he insisted she only had to be shown once. There was a great deal of affection between them both and he insisted that collar restraint and a firm "NO" were the only negative requirements in the field of training dogs. Rewards for obedience and a severe "telling off" for disobedience were quickly understood, he said. Beatings and other punishments were totally unnecessary in a good partnership.

He was, in fact, a confirmed bachelor and that may account for the success of his partnership with Pickles.

"She can't answer back and she does as she's told," he informed us. "She goes where I go and doesn't poke her nose in which is more than can be said of some wives."

Brumby was somewhat of a loner. He liked to fish for coarse fish and he had a passion for eels which he usually "jellied up" with a cod's head from the local fish shop. He was, I'm sure, happiest without company and although he frequented the local pub and talked to all and sundry he would seldom accept a "treat". Invariably his reply, when asked, would be "No thanks, I'm not stopping long." None of which suggests he did not enjoy conversing with his fellow men. Quite the reverse was true at times.

He lived, as I was led to understand, with a widowed sister and her two young children. He regarded their well-being as his first priority and saw to it that they were well supplied with game throughout the winter months. World War II had been over for some time but meat was still on ration and a brace or two of mallard duck were welcomed by any meat-hungry housewife so favoured.

"She can't cook worth a damn," said Brumby of his sister, "but even she finds it hard to spoil a roast duck. If she remembers to put it in and pull it out at the right time not much can go wrong."

He plucked and dressed the birds himself and, as he put it, "left the rest to providence."

Brumby had not only a love for wild duck as table produce but also a great understanding of how and where to acquire them.

"You'll find no shot in my ducks," he would boast. "Shooting's too uncertain. My way's guaranteed and doesn't rely on lead poisoning."

It was true that his wild duck appeared only ever to have had their necks wrung. We shared amenities occasionally and I never found lead pellets in any duck Brumby ever gave to me.

He claimed to be a specialist and it is very true that he knew his quarry. He knew the times and the places well. He could assess when flights would arrive and he was an expert at feeding. Not a single rabbit paunch was wasted when Brumby had ducks in mind. He knew that rabbit entrails held a fatal attraction for mallard and teal and he placed them strategically at the appropriate time in the appropriate places. Had he been a sporting shooter he could have conjured up the finest evening flight shooting that it is possible to envisage but he was, in fact, a pot-hunter pure and simple. There was also a hint of doubt about the legality of his flight feeds! His evening flight ventures were seldom considered until evening had become night. They coincided with a certain phase of the moon and more often than not depended upon his silent and stealthy all night vigil.

It depended exactly upon his requirements at the time. He tried for the most part not to over-crop his sources and when he employed his unique duck trapping system he was able (or so he claimed) to take what he needed and release the rest unharmed. This, he said, could not be practised with birds that had been shot. A dead duck had no escape clause, he insisted.

His duck trap was a simple wire netting affair that could be collapsed and concealed in a double hedgerow without drawing the attention of anyone passing close to it. It had, as Brumby put it, an easy way in and a nigh impossible way out. Based on the simple live trap principle wherein the quarry negotiates a tunnel entrance to reach a food supply, it was set up on dry land very close to the water's edge. Food was scattered around and inside the trap and the entrance via the tunnel ensured that the ducks were trapped. The only difference between Brumby's trap and many other live traps was that, by a series of pegs and split rings, it could be collapsed to lie flat on the ground.

Its rusty exterior was hardly worth a second glance and a few dead leaves scattered here and there camouflaged it completely. Its effectiveness depended upon a regular feeding procedure before the final setting and the success of Brumby's many illicit ventures could be recognised in the numbers of duck he produced several times during a season. He made it quite clear, to those of us who asked, that he would never exploit a water more than once a month. That way, he said, he had half a dozen prime opportunities each year on each water. To trap more often than that was greedy *and* impracticable, he insisted. I believed him when he told me he had often caught a dozen ducks but only retained half of them. The released birds, he said, would eventually come back with the others on later flights.

Not all his duck hunting methods were quite that humane, however. When Brumby needed meat he offered no quarter. In those days of meat shortage I understood his methods even if I could not, in honesty, defend them. They involved the use of a quantity of boiled "lights" (as fed to the family moggie) and that is all I will say about it. In those days of meat shortage it was, perhaps, reasonable to adopt an "anything goes" philosophy. To use Brumby's methods today would be unthinkable.

There came a time when Brumby's haul was surplus to his requirements and his subsequent visit to the butcher saw him return with a substantial chunk of genuine fillet steak. He talked of it the same evening and drooled as he described the feast that was to be his to share with his sister and two hungry youngsters next day. We, who had not seen fillet steak for many years, envied his droolings.

From the tales that have been told since, it would appear that Brumby talked to his workmates for most of the next day about his forthcoming sumptuous repast. It would be seared and sealed in a hot skillet so that the succulent, pink inner part would retain its nutrition and flavour. Crusty new bread, hot English mustard, onions and chips would enhance this meal fit for a king and Brumby would again reign supreme as the breadwinner of all time.

It has to be said that the lady of the house had never before seen fillet steak. She had been presented, to all intents and purposes, with a chunk of beef that had to be cooked for next day's evening meal. And not knowing the finer points of beef cookery she diced it all and turned it into a beef casserole which she cooked slowly in a thick gravy. Excellent for cheaper and tougher cuts of beef but somewhat wasted on expensive fillet steak.

There was an odd look on Brumby's face as he called for his ale at the local that night. Those present should have noticed. They ought not to have asked but they did.

"How was the steak then, Brumby?"

A single tear came to Brumby's eye and a wild look came over his face. He choked back a sob.

"She b'iled it," he said. "She bloody b'iled it!"